COMPACT
CYMRU

CW00498454

Old Bridges of Snowdonia

Des Marshall

Gwasg Carreg Gwalch

First published in 2021
© text & photos: Des Marshall
Publication: Gwasg Carreg Gwalch

ISBN: 978-1-84524-394-4
Cover design: Eleri Owen

Published by Gwasg Carreg Gwalch,
12 Iard yr Orsaf, Llanrwst, Wales LL26 0EH
tel: 01492 642031
email: books@carreg-gwalch.cymru
website: www.carreg-gwalch.cymru

Pont Llechwedd Hafod in Cwm Penmachno.

Contents

LIST OF OTHER BRIDGES MARKED ON THE OS MAPS Not being described

BONT-DDU   SH 669 186
BONT NEWYDD   SH 881 379 over
    the Nant Aberbleidoyn
BONT NEWYDD   SH 757 673
    above Dolgarrog
BONT NEWYDD   SH 714 409
    Llan Ffestiniog
BONT NEWYDD   SH 810 534
*FIGRA BRIDGE   SH 667 191
PONT ABERDUNANT   SH 589 418
PONT ABERGWYNANT   SH 678 171
PONT AFON FECHAN   SH 883 288
PONT AR BYLAN   SH 766 160
PONT AR GELYN   SH 844 418
PONT AR BUMRYD   SH 904 191
PONT BALADEULYN   SH 511 534
PONT BANCOG   SH 828 532
PONT BLAEN LLIW   SH 801 334
PONT BORTHWNOG   SH 689 191
PONTBREN TITW   SH 809 220
PONT BUARTHMEINI   SH 826 325
PONT CALETWR   SH 600 110
PONT CAE NEWYDD   SH 632 313
PONT CAE'R GORS   SH 575 508
PONT CEFN COCH   SH 765 175
PONT CERRIG   SH 634 261
PONT CRAFNANT   SH 617 289
PONT CWM NANTCOL   SH 616 268
PONT CWM YR AFON   SH 621 298

PONT DOLGARROG   SH 774 663
PONT DOLORGAN   SH 621 356
PONT DÔL-Y-BONT   SH 860 151
PONT DÔL Y MYNACH   SH 733 311
PONT DOLYDD PRYSOR   SH 745 361
PONT PANT EIDAL   SH 660 972
PONT EIDDA   SH 834 504
PONT ELEN   SH 765 457
PONT EVANS   SH 755 060
PONT FELINRHYD FAWR   SH 653 395
PONT FFRIDD DDU   SH 661 204
PONT FRONWYDD   SH 831 245
PONT FUCHES WEN   SH 606 349
PONT GARTH GELL   SH 684 205
PONT HAFOD DYWYLL   SH 684 159
PONT IAGO   SH 690 077
PONT KINGS   SH 683 160
PONT LLANRHAEADR   SH 794 209
PONT MWNWGL Y LLYN   SH 929 351 Bala
PONT NANT Y LLADRON   SH 779 397
PONT NANT Y DUGOED   SH 917 132
PONT NANT YR EHEDYDD   SH 908 127
PONT NEWYDD   SH 758 671
   above Dolgarrog
PONT NEWYDD   SH 861 512
PONT OERNANT   SH 785 494
PONT PANT GWYN   SH 851 273
PONT PEN Y BEDW   SH 780 486
PONT PEN Y BONT   SH 783 489
PONT PEN Y BONT   SH 607 280
PONT PEN Y BONT   SH 871 306
PONT RHYD-DDWL   SH 797 215

PONT RHYD GOCH   SH 678 604
PONT RHYD-SARN   SH 858 286
PONT RHYD-Y-MEIRCH   SH 762 477
PONT RHYD-Y-FEN   SH 819 393
PONT TAFARN HELYG   SH 687 397
PONT TALARDD   SH 894 269
PONT TALYRNI   SH 608 446
PONT TRAWSYFNYDD   SH 709 350
PONT TŶ-GWYN   SH 681 165
PONT TY'N Y DDÔL   SH 914 382
PONT WALTON   SH 847 097
PONT WEN   SH 736 227
PONT WENFFRWD   SH 607 992
PONT WERN GOF   SH 673 605
PONT WRYSGEN   SH 870 130
PONT Y DDÔL   SH 531 454
PONT Y DDÔL   SH 763 710
PONT Y BALA   SH 929 362
PONT Y BYLAN   SH 765 160
PONT Y CLEIFION   SH 861 127
PONT Y COBLYN   SH 719 515
PONT Y FELINDRE   SH 614 031
PONT Y FOEL   SH 764 479
PONT Y GLYN   SH 609 345
PONT Y GRIBLE   SH 708 304
PONT Y GROMLECH   SH 629 565
PONT Y LLAFAR   SH 893 324
PONT Y PANDY   SH 880 297 Llanuwchllyn
PONT Y PENNANT   SH 904 202
PONT Y PLAS   SH 529 459
PONT YSTUMANNER   SH 660 078
STABLAU BONT   SH 718 580

Introduction

Very little was written about bridges until 1926 when an Edward Jervoise set about recording all he considered 'ancient'. It took him six years to complete this monumental task when he visited some 5,000. During 1931/32 Jervoise visited all the bridges he considered ancient in Wales and the west of England. In 1936 he published 'Ancient Bridges of Wales and the West of England' detailing his findings which was the last in the series. Some 300 of these were scheduled ancient. A facsimile copy was published in 1876 by the publishers E.P.

The earliest bridges were probably fallen trees slippery when wet and only really suitable for humans to cross whilst Neolithic people built a type of boardwalk across boggy ground. Stepping stones can be classed as a type, but very basic form, of bridge and evolved from an early age. They were possibly the earliest forms that enabled the crossing flowing water. These were superseded by another ancient form known as 'clapper bridges'. Dating back to prehistoric times these are the earliest type of constructed bridge. They are found in considerable numbers in all the mountainous areas of Britain especially in Snowdonia and the Lake District. Large flat slabs of local stone, especially in slate quarrying areas, were supported by stone piers situated in larger streams or, perhaps, to enable the crossing of a small stream just one slab was placed that rested on each of the banks. These bridges allowed carts either drawn by horses or pushed by people to easily cross. It also allowed farmers to drive their animals more safely. They did not have any type of guard rail.

The greatest builders of early bridges were the Romans. Their style of building were of arch construction and included aqueducts. They were infinitely stronger than the earlier forms with some still standing today. Some of the bridges that were built when turnpike roads started to be constructed were sited close to fords, notably the one in Dolbenmaen.

In Medieval times and up to the mid-18th century most bridges were constructed from wood. In those days motor transport did not exist and only needed to support the weight of horse, carts and later on stagecoaches. They were easy to build and were able to be repaired quickly or even replaced when damaged or washed away by flooding. Unfortunately no wooden bridge survives of any great age although the bridge at Penmaenpool and the railway bridge spanning Afon Mawddach are constructed predominantly from wood. There are however many wooden footbridges of no age at all. One striking footbridge is the Miners Bridge close to Betws-y-coed, but this again is a replacement of several earlier ones.

The idea of crossing deep gorges or ravines by suspension bridges also evolved. The original type of a single rope for the feet and one for each hand was quickly superseded by much safer designs as flooring was introduced. Eventually as tools and equipment improved stone bridges started to be built from the late 1700's although, as mentioned above, some stone bridges had been built much earlier. After the Romans departed there are some records of stone built bridges being built from the 13th century.

The great breakthrough of stone built bridges came with the perfection of constructing arches. Solid foundations were needed and what better example of these than at Pont-y-pair in Betws-y-coed. Early on, arch building was a skill that only

a few mastered. 'Formers' were needed and were constructed by the carpenter, a very important person indeed for the construction. Constructing the former was often the most difficult and dangerous task, especially if it was being built across a fast flowing and deep river or a high gorge. In multi arch bridges piers were first of all constructed up to the height of the arch. Whilst the arch was being built another pier would be built for the next arch. Once the 'arch rings' had been built a temporary roadway was laid using planks.

The first layer of stones built over the former are known as 'arch rings'. Sometimes these were laid in two layers and termed 'double arch rings'. The arch is held in position by the 'keystone', a wedge shaped stone placed in the centre of the arch. The building of the arch ring and placing of the keystone were vitally important to the strength of the bridge. Pressure from above the arch forces the keystone down thus keeping the arch secure, although if there is too much pressure the weight on the 'spandrels' (haunches) forces the keystone to upwards. This would cause the bridge to collapse!

Bridges without 'parapets' are rare. They are all that stops carts, animals, vehicles, people from getting a severe wetting or being dashed to death on the rocks below. They can vary in height from a few inches or centimetres to 6 feet or 1.8 metres.

A 'cutwater' is an essential feature of piers. They are usually pointed and look like the bow of a ship and erected on the upstream side of the bridge to part water as it flows through the arch. If the cutwater reached the roadway it was possible to create a refuge, especially important on bridges where stagecoaches sped across. Triangular in shape they allowed pedestrians to take refuge and sometimes they had seats. A good example of this is found at Pont Dôl-y-moch. Usually though cutwaters ended half way up the pier.

Arches are described by whatever part of a circle they form. For example segmented or semi circular. very few arches were pointed. In the early days stone bridges often took four or five years to build. This being due to the fact that work could only be carried out in the summer when water levels were usually low. Some of the bridges in Snowdonia were constructed over boulder strewn rivers and it was difficult to find solid foundations. As such they have different size arches.

I have highlighted a couple of good examples of 'clapper bridges' in the text. A selection of stepping stone crossings are included as are a couple of railway bridges and a suspension footbridge, although this is only for private access. Interestingly a number of boardwalks have been constructed in recent years across boggy ground, no doubt inspired by the Neolithic builders!

The bridges described herein can all be found by looking at the relevant Ordnance Survey maps. The best ones to use are 1:25,000 Explorer series. The maps pertaining to this book are: OL 17 Snowdon/Yr Wyddfa, OL 18 Harlech, Porthmadog & Bala/Y Bala, OL 23 Cadair Idris & Llyn Tegid and OL 254 Lleyn Peninsula East/Pen Llyn Ardal Ddwyreiniol. When visiting these bridges it is sensible to use a nearby car park or lay-by. Avoid stopping on the bridge. Not only does this restrict free movement of traffic it is usually not the best position to view them. Very little walking is required to see them. One marvels at the construction of these old bridges and how they have remained in use for several centuries. Some of the older ones have had new counterparts built. For example the ones at Pont Minllyn and Llanelltyd. These new bridges are nowhere near as attractive and in my opinion they have no character whatsoever.

The act of jumping off a bridge, known as 'tomb-stoning', is very dangerous. Limbs are often broken as hidden rocks or large trees lurk below water level. Trees can also trap the jumper and then being unable to surface death quickly follows! Water is often very cold as the rivers emanate from high colder mountain areas and a sudden immersion can also bring about heart failure. many of the bridges can be seen from the river it spans. Be mindful though that the approaches are often steep, loose and riddled with brambles. So TAKE CARE and have fun visiting these old places and enjoy.

NOTE: True left and true right are the correct terms used when looking downstream.

Parts of a bridge

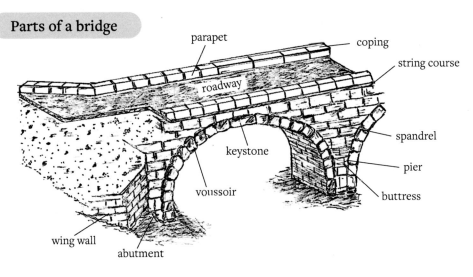

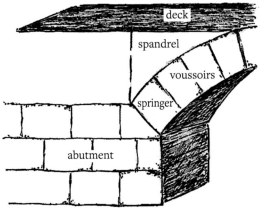

General
Location
Map

Ynys Môn
(Anglesey)

Llandudno

A55 Conwy

Afon
Conwy

Bangor

Bethesda

A470

Caernarfon

A4085 A4086

A487

Llanrwst

A5

Betws-y-coed

Llanberis

A498

Beddgelert

Blaenau
Ffestiniog

A4212

Porthmadog

SNOWDONIA

Y Bala

Harlech

Afon
Mawddach

A470

A494

A496

Bermo
(Barmouth)

Dolgellau

A493

A487

Afon
Dyfi

A470

Tywyn

A489

Aberdyfi

Machynlleth

Old Bridges of Snowdonia 11

BARMOUTH BRIDGE
(Pont y Bermo/Pont Abermaw)

Map: Ordnance Survey 1:25,000 Explorer series OL 23 Cadair Idris & Llyn Tegid
Grid reference: SH 622 151

This iconic structure spans the Mawddach Estuary and carries the railway line from Pwllheli to Machynlleth. and is one of the longest timber viaducts still standing in the UK today. It is a Grade 11 listed structure some 2,300 feet or 699 metres long, consisting of 113 timber trestles supported by a series of cast iron pillars. It was designed by Benjamin Piercy and Henry Conybeare in 1864. Taking 3 years to build it was opened on the 10th October 1867. Conybeare shipped the timber in as it was much cheaper to do so than iron. When it was first built there was a lifting drawbridge at the northern end to allow the tall ships of the day to pass up the river. However, since the railway opened there was little call for it so in 1899 it was altered to a swing bridge. Although still theoretically operational it has not been opened since 1987 when it was last tested!

Little is known of the history of Barmouth or, in Welsh, Abermaw but sometimes colloquially Bermo as often seen on the local busses. The dominating hill to the north of the town known as Dinas Oleu, (dinas: stronghold; (g)oleu: light) was settled by the Romans. Many of the scattered farmhouses date back to the 15th century whilst the older buildings in the old part of town date back to the 17th. Barmouth developed around shipbuilding until 1865, although very little if anything at all remains of this once thriving industry. Once trains arrived in 1867 shipbuilding declined very quickly. Barmouth has been dubbed 'Queen of the Cambrian Coast'.

Visitors to the area included Charles Darwin, Percy Bysshe Shelley, and George Byron. William Wordsworth visited Barmouth in the 19th century saying: 'With a fine sea view in front, the mountains behind, the glorious estuary running eight miles inland and Cadair Idris 2,930 feet or 893 metres within compass of a day's walk, Barmouth can always hold its own against any rival'. They came no doubt inspired by the works of Thomas Pennant 1726 – 1798.

Barmouth Bridge from the slopes of Dinas Oleu.

BEAVER BRIDGE (Pont yr Afanc)

Map: Ordnance Survey 1:25,000 Explorer series OL 18 Harlech, Porthmadog & Bala/Y Bala
Grid reference: SH 798 546

Not named on the OS map. The bridge spans Afon Conwy close to Betws y coed. Although Beaver Bridge is the usual name used nowadays it is properly called Pont yr Afanc. The bridge itself carries the main arterial road through Wales, the A470. This starts in Cardiff and continues all the way to Llandudno. Beaver Bridge is set a beautiful position close to, but downstream of Fairy Falls. It was probably built in 1803 by the sons of a local inn keeper whose inn was situated on the site of today's railway station. At one time it carried the main road to Betws-y-coed before Waterloo Bridge was built in 1815. The span is 68 feet or 20.7 metres by a single, almost semicircular arch. Apparently the first person to cross the bridge was a Mr Wynne who crossed it in a four wheeled carriage.

He was a world renowned naturalist and antiquary encouraging people to visit Wales.

Once known as the Maw the Mawddach Estuary was first mentioned in the 12th century by the traveller Geraldus Cambrensis. He was a cleric who went around trying to enlist people for the Crusades.

The pool downstream of the bridge is known as Llyn yr Afanc (*'beaver pool'*) and one of many moods. In spring and summer sunlight sparkles across the ripples of water but on a dark moody winter's day the pool presents a different face being foreboding, mysterious and sombre. Salmon have been observed in the water here. Upstream close to the site of the bridge was an ancient ford called Rhyd y Gwyniedyn. The name for the pool is steeped in Welsh folklore. Many, many years ago beavers once did live in the pool.

However, there was also a huge giant of one, It was hunted by the local people but was unable to be killed because its skin was so tough the arrows and spears just bounced off. As many other of these legends are told a fair maiden was summoned to sing to it from the river bank.

True to form the Beaver rose from the depths and enchanted listened to the maiden's dulcet voice until being lulled into sleep. The hunters came with their nets and ropes and captured it. With two oxen the beast was dragged all the way to Llyn Glaslyn below Snowdon where it was released and slid below the water never to be seen again!

1. Barmouth Bridge looking towards Cadair Idris; 2. Barmouth Bridge looking upstream; 3. Beaver Bridge looking downstream.

BONT FAWR (Dolgellau Bridge)

Map: Ordnance Survey 1:25,000 Explorer series OL 23 Cadair Idris & Llyn Tegid and OL 18 Harlech, Porthmadog & Bala/Y Bala
Grid reference: SH 728 180

Named as Dolgellau Bridge on the OS map it is today a bridge of seven arches spanning Afon Wnion. Although very little of the original bridge is visible nowadays this bridge is considered, perhaps, as one of the oldest in the area. Many sections have been repaired over the years. Only the downstream portion of the middle three arches are original. Originally it was a bridge of 10 arches but reduced to seven when the railway was built. According to one traveller, a certain Jervoise, in 1931, the inscription A. D. 1638 was still legible on one of the southern arches. He mentioned also that the original width was only 11feet or 3.3 metres. This was obviously sufficient for horses and carts. The bridge was widened during rebuilding to 15 feet or 4.6 metres whilst the length is 70 yards or 64 metres.

The bridge is somewhat unique in that it was built on a slant to overcome the different heights of the riverbanks. The two southern arches are almost silted up.

Dolgellau means *'meadows of the cells'* in English which, perhaps, pertains that there were monastic cells here at one time. Owain Glyndŵr who had a Parliament in Machynlleth from 1402 held an assembly in the town in 1404 on the site of T. H. Roberts shop. It became the main town of the old county of Meirionnydd in the 16th century. During the 18th and 19th centuries Dolgellau had a large woollen industry specialising in flannel, as did Machynlleth, and was used for soldier's uniforms. The town has perhaps the highest proportion of listed buildings of anywhere in Wales with over 200. It became a conservation area in 1991.

A local folk story says that a fairy once lived in a pool under the bridge. After she married Hugh Evans, a local man, she told him not to follow her. One night frustrated as to where she went he followed her. Whilst stalking her he fell and broke his leg. His wife tended him until he was able to walk again and then vanished forever!

1.& 2. Bont Fawr,
Dolgellau upstream view.

BONT NEWYDD

Map: Ordnance Survey 1:25,000 Explorer series OL 17 Snowdon/Yr Wyddfa
Grid reference: SH 662 719

Situated above Abergwyngregyn close to the A55 Bangor to Conwy road the bridge is marked as an antiquity on the OS map as well as in regular typeface. It spans the Afon Aber and was built no earlier than the mid 18th century and has a single segmented arch of 15 yards or 13.7 metres and a width of 13 feet or 3.9 metres. There is a car park nearby for a starting point for the walk up to the iconic Rhaeadr Fawr, Aber Falls.

Abergwyngregyn, although small, is an interesting and a historically important little village. A large, grassy, circular mound is very prominent and is known as Llywelyn's Mound. However, it more than likely predated Llywelyn by over six hundred years being built around the 5th or 6th century and possibly above the body of a champion warrior.

The tower in the village, seen when descending the steep path, is known as Tŵr Llywelyn and built about A.D. 1200. It is reputed to be the home of Llywelyn ap Gruffudd, Prince of Wales and Lord of Snowdon. A secret chamber below the tower reputedly has a tunnel that runs from the house, now known as Garth Celyn, under the Menai Strait to Anglesey. Legend also has it that the horse belonging to Prince Llywelyn was hitched to a post in this cellar in readiness for him to ride out to fight the English.

1. Bont Newydd, Abergwyngregyn downstream side;
2 Pont Newydd. SH 861 512.

BONT NEWYDD

Map: Ordnance Survey 1:25,000 Explorer series OL 23 Cadair Idris & Llyn Tegid
Grid reference: SH 771 201

This bridge, spanning Afon Wnion, carries the B4416 down from Brithdir to the junction with the A494 Dolgellau to Bala. Although listed as an antiquity the bridge has been repaired and widened on the upstream side to 16 feet or 4.9 metres. Unfortunately it is almost impossible to date the age as the underneath has been cemented over hiding the original stonework. That said the situation is very pretty. The 14 feet or 4.27 metres wide is between the 2 feet 5 inches or 74 centimetres high parapet. Intermittent copings are from concrete or stone.

CLAPPER BRIDGES

(1) Map: Ordnance Survey 1:25,000 Explorer series OL 17 Snowdon/Yr Wyddfa
Grid reference: SH 539 492

The example of a 'clapper bridge' shown here is one of simple form and is situated at the end of the tarmac road in Cwm Pennant. This small span lays across the infant Afon Dwyfor and used for pedestrian access to Dôl Ifan Gethin, a now abandoned and derelict house. In times of high water the ford at the end of the road, nowadays raised from its original state, would have been too dangerous to cross on foot. The bridge is now defunct but remains as a reminder of times past.

(2) Map: Ordnance Survey 1:25,000 Explorer series OL 23 Cadair Idris & Llyn Tegid
Grid reference: above Arthog Waterfalls SH 648 138

The one shown here is in two spans across Afon Arthog, which has split at this point before joining again, beyond the top of Arthog Falls and is easily reached by the attractive walk up past the waterfalls.

1. *Bont Newydd, Brithdir, looking upstream;*
2. *Clapper bridges across Afon Dwyfor, at the head of Cwm Pennant;*
3. *Clapper bridges across Afon Arthog above the waterfalls*

(3) **Map:** Ordnance Survey 1:25,000 series OL 18 Harlech, Porthmadog & Bala/Y Bala **Grid reference:** SH 639 452

Spanning Afon Croesor this fine clapper bridge carried the Croesor Tramway from the head of Cwm Croesor to Porthamdog. It was opened in 1864.The tramway is 8 miles long and had a gauge of 2 feet or .6 metre. Croesor and Rhosydd slate mines were connected to it via two separate and impressive single pitch inclines. They were the longest in Wales with each descending 750 feet or 229 metres. A quarter mile beyond the base of the inclines they descended another 150 feet or 46 metres down the Blaen y Cwm incline to the valley floor. The tramway then followed this to Croesor village crossing on its way three fine clapper bridges. One of these is pictured here.

1. Clapper bridges, this one carried the Croesor Tramway over the Afon Croesor;
2. Clapper bridges, single span example below Moel Isallt, Cwmystradllyn;
3. Clapper bridges across the Afon y Cwm, Craflwyn.

(4) **Map:** Ordnance Survey 1:25,000 series OL 254 Lleyn Peninsula East/Pen Llŷn Ardal Ddwyeiniol **Grid reference:** SH 543 446

Situated above Cwmystradllyn and below the fine viewpoint of Moel Isallt this a perfect example of a single span clapper bridge. Spanning a narrow but deep ditch it was wide enough for horse and cart it allows modern day farm vehicles to cross as the slabs of slate are over 4 inches or 10 millimetres thick. Supported by constructed stone pillars three slate slabs are laid side by side. It is well worth seeking out and is crossed on a right of way from the lane leading to and past Traian on the pleasant walk to the summit of Moel Isallt.

There are other examples of 'clapper' or 'slab' bridges in Snowdonia. One of these is the one spanning the Afon Cwm Llan leading from the Watkin Path to access Cwm Meirch whilst another (pictured) is the one over the Afon y Cwm crossed on the walk from Craflwyn to Dinas Emrys.

IVY BRIDGE

Map: Ordnance Survey 1:25,000 Explorer series OL 18 Harlech, Porthmadog & Bala/Y Bala
Grid reference: SH 654 394

An 18th century bridge. Some reports suggest that it is 700 years old! It spans Afon Prysor on the old route from Maentwrog to Harlech and is very aptly named as ivy drapes itself over the side of the bridge not unlike ragged curtains to almost reach the river. It is 6 feet or 1.8 metres wide and is constructed from roughly coursed rubble stonework. There is a single segmented arch with rough stone voussoirs. There is no parapet! However, it is possible to walk across the rough surface on the right of way.

A walk is required to view this ancient structure but it is well worth the slight amount of effort. The 300 metres walk through woodland is best done from a large lay-by on the A496 on the Maentwrog side of Pont Felenrhyd fawr, itself an interesting bridge with Moelwyn Bach 2,329 feet or 710 metres high as a backdrop. Upstream a woodland walk leads to Rhaeadr Du.

The hydro electric Maentwrog Power Station was constructed in 1928 by Sir Alexander Gibb and Partners for the North Wales Power Co. Ltd. It still generates electricity today. Water arrives here down massive pipes from Llyn Trawsfynydd,

Maentwrog literally means Twrog's stone. According to a legend a giant going by the name of Twrog hurled a boulder from the top of the hill above the settlement. The result being that it destroyed a pagan altar. It is said that the very stone is the one found in the churchyard by the church porch. measuring 4 feet or 1.2 metres high is not from the locally found rock and is of glacial origin. The indents found at the top of the stone are said to be the prints of the giant's thumb and finger. Another legend from the Mabinogion, stories of pre-

Christian Celtic mythology, says that Pryderi was killed by Gwydion at Afon Glasyn and is buried in Maentwrog.

The village church is dedicated to an eminent Welsh Saint St Twrog. He lived close by at the end of the 5th century and beginning of the 6th. The church seen today was built in 1814 on the site of the original.

1. *Pont Felenrhyd Fawr looking downstream from opposite maentwrog power station. Moelwyn Bach is in the background; 2. Ivy Bridge draped with Ivy; 3. Ivy Bridge showing the path over the hump.*

LODGE BRIDGE

Map: Ordnance Survey 1:25,000 Explorer Series OL 254 Lleyn Peninsula East/Pen Llŷn Ardal Ddwyeiniol
Grid reference: SH 519 433

This old bridge carrying a minor road and spanning Afon Dwyfor in its middle section gives access from the lower section of Cwm Pennant to the Brithdir Hall and Estate. It could well have been built with this in mind. Brynkir Tower can be seen poking its turreted tower above the trees.

This was originally a folly built as a celebration of the personal success of Sir Joseph Huddart, a millionaire, of Brynkir House. He was knighted in 1821 the same year that George the 4th was crowned king. However, it provided work for the local craftsmen in the slump immediately after the Napoleonic Wars. It has been said that Huddart was knighted for his services to industry as well as mine enterprises. These last were not that successful and he landed himself in dire financial straits. He was a friend of William Alexander Madocks who built the rather more useful Cob at Porthmadog.

Today, having fallen into disrepair and becoming a shell, the six storey Rapunzel like tower has been restored by its present owner. The floors had collapsed and it was possible to see all the way up from floor to roof. Thankfully CADW, a Welsh Heritage organisation, came to the rescue as the structure was a grade II listed building. The tower is now back to its former glory and is now let as holiday accommodation. The views across to Hendre Ddu slate quarry and to Cwm Pennant from the grounds are excellent as is the view towards Moel Hebog.

Robert Wynn was the first to adopt Brynkir as a family name in 1563. James Brynkir is buried in the graveyard of St Michael's church in Llanfihangel-y-pennant having died in 1644. His headstone bears the name Brynkir. At the end of the 19th century the Brynkir estate collapsed, mainly due to the cost of the upkeep of the place. The mansion house had its heyday in the 16th and 17th centuries. Successive owners built what became a tangle of rooms. As one part became uninhabitable another new wing was built! The walls were built from the rock at Craig Gyfyng.

Lodge Bridge, Cwm Pennant.

In '*Lost House of Wales*' by Thomas Lloyd there is an amazing photograph of Brynkir although much of what is seen in the photo has disappeared.

The house grew into a monster with many long passages leading to unwanted rooms. The place was abandoned, so the story goes, at a moment's notice! The house remained intact having been so well built and was used to house German prisoners of war at the end of WWI. The still well stocked wine cellar was broken into by the prisoners one night so no doubt they had one hell of a boozy session! The bottles had all been personalised by a glass seal bearing the inscription Brynkir. The final breakup of the Estate which had lasted for 400 years came on the afternoon of Friday 25th April 1930. Today the ruins are hidden in a tangle of trees, bushes and nettles. Close to the ruins is a large stone building that was once the stables for the mansion. Until recently this was the Cwm Pennant Outdoor Centre.

Joseph Huddart owned Brynkir Mansion from 1809 and there are reports that he was undertaking repairs in 1812 and introducing a marble chimney piece, a kitchen grate, floors and putting in laths for a ceiling. He spent most of his time away from the place living in Highbury Place, London. As well as rebuilding Brynkir, Huddart undertook the complete development of the demesne, land surrounding the house, and Home Farm. The lower part of the valley was designed as a park and the wild slopes tamed and converted into smooth grassland planted here and there with clumps of trees. By 1823 the low hill above the mansion was crowned with a tower. Rocks on the hillside were cleared and built into fine walls. This created rich pasture land. Trees were planted everywhere both in single rows and in thick groves. These protected the cattle and crops. Farm buildings were also erected. Leats were built to bring water, not only for drinking purposes but also to provide power to small waterwheels that in turn powered the churns and dairies in those farms. Harvests were notoriously bad during the depression immediately after the Napoleonic Wars.

PENMAENPOOL BRIDGE

Map: Ordnance Survey 1:25,000 Explorer series OL 23 Cadair Idris & Llyn Tegid
Grid reference: SH 694 185

This remarkable bridge was built in 1880 by the Penmaenpool Bridge Company Limited in ana agreement made with the Barmouth Harbour Trust. It is still privately owned and spans the Afon Mawddach providing a 'short cut' between Barmouth and Fairbourne. A small charge is made to cross during its usual opening hours from 08.30 to 18.30. The toll in 2019 was .70 p per car or .20p for a pedestrian. Any vehicle weighing over 1.5 tons are not permitted to cross. Tolls are collected on the southern side of the bridge from the toll booth adjacent to the bridge owners house.

The bridge spans are of 20 feet or 16.4 metres with a central one of 30 feet or 10.9 metres. This was designed to allow for an opening section if ever larger boats were built upstream if ever the disused boat building yards were ever re-opened. They didn't so it was it was never required. The

1. Penmaenpool Bridge looking upstream;
2. Penmaenpool Bridge road deck.

construction is a series of timber trestles with a heavy deck of diagonally baulk timbers. Although solid and secure some of the decking boards rattle when driven over!

The bridge is very close to the George III hotel on the celebrated Mawddach Trail with the old station and platform now part of the hotel. The trail is the track-bed of the former railway line from Barmouth to Ruabon. The old signal box is now a bird watchers' hide.

The George III dates back to circa1650. It was in two halves at that time with one half being a pub and the other a ship's chandlers for the thriving ship building industry. Around 1890 the two halves were joined to form the hotel. The lodge, a Victorian building, was erected to form a waiting room, ticket office and the station master's house for the adjacent station by Cambrian Railways the original owner of the line before being taken over by Great Western railway in 1922. The line closed in 1965 courtesy of Dr Beeching's axe! It was acquired by the hotel in 1977. Gerald Manley Hopkins is reputed to have written a poem in one of the old guest books. Titled 'Penmaenpool' the first four lines read:

'Then come who pine for peace and
pleasure,
Away from counter, court and school,
Spend here your measure of time and
treasure,
And taste the treats of Penmaenpool'.

Five years prior to the railway arriving in 1865 Penmaenpool was an estate village. It had a row of terraced cottages serving a model farm which in turn served Penmaenucha Hall. This was the country residence of a Bolton cotton magnate. Before the railway, ship building flourished. Interestingly, ships were launched sideways into the circular 'pool' by drink fuelled locals who had been plied with free booze. In 1862 the last ship to be built here was named 'Charlotte'.

An interesting notice on the signal outside the hotel says 'DANGER survivors will be prosecuted'.

A great tragedy unfolded at the bridge at 10,55 on the 22nd July 1966. It was the first day of the school summer holidays. The *Prince of Wales* pleasure boat left Barmouth for the regular two hour return sail to Penmaenpool. It was carrying the captain and 42 passengers. As it arrived and turned into the jetty it hit

Penmaenpool Bridge. This sadly ended with the boat sinking with 15 passengers losing their lives.

The proprietor of the George III at that time was John A. Hall. He launched his own nine foot long rowing boat called *The Daisy May* which he had only bought five days beforehand. Along with two of his employees David Christopher Jones and Robert Jones they saved many lives. Another rescuer was Ronald Phillip Davies an employee of the local District Council. He waded into the river on two occasions and saved the lives of two children.

PONT ABERGEIRW

Map: 1:25,000 Ordnance Survey Explorer Series OL 23 Cadair Idris & Llyn Tegid
Grid reference: SH 768 291

This remote bridge of unknown age spans the infant Afon Mawddach. It has long abutments with two square flood openings on the southern or downstream side on the true left of the river. The parapets are 3 feet 3 inches or 1 metre high between which is the 12 feet 6 inches or 3.81 metres road. When viewed from below the bridge has noticeably new and old sections. At some time in the not too distant past the bridge has been widened to accommodate the road.

> 1. *Pont Abergeirw looking upstream;*
> 2. *Pont Abergeirw underside view of the old and new.*

PONT ABERGLASLYN

Map: Ordnance Survey 1:25,000 Explorer series OL 17 Snowdon/Yr Wyddfa
Grid reference: SH 594 462

Originally built in the 17th century the bridge was widened and its height increased around 1795/96. The bridge spans the attractive stretch of Afon Glaslyn as it flows through the Abergladlyn Gorge. A walk up the Fisherman's Path is delightful but demands care, especially in

high water conditions. In 1957 during restoration work the original bridge was revealed having been incorporated into the present one. Inscribed on the parapet the initials WM along with the date of 1656. An inscription '*Ric thom e Col Jes*' was also discovered which indicated that they belonged to Richard Thomas of Jesus College.

The bridge is 50 feet or 15 metres long constructed from rubble with a wide segmented arch. Rough dressed voussoirs are recessed below the narrow arch stones. The upstream side has a plain, flat string course below the parapet whilst the downstream side the voussoirs are longer and the string course gently pointed above the arch. The road, the A4085, is level but the parapet with flat coping stones, curves with the road at the eastern end. At the west end of the bridge are milestones dating from the late 19th century or early 20th. The on the downstream parapet is inscribed To Porthmadog 6 miles whilst on the upstream side are two milestones. One is inscribed To Beddgelert 1¼ miles and the other To Penrhyndeudraeth 6 miles.

There is a fable attached to this bridge but similar stories exist for other bridges in the UK. A notable one being Devil's Bridge near Aberystwyth. The version for Pont Aberglaslyn is that the Devil built it on the understanding that he would take the soul of the first living creature to cross. After building was finished he went to the local pub to inform a local magician, Robin Ddu, that it was completed. Robin went to the bridge along with a dog. This had been lured by a loaf of freshly baked bread. When they had all reached the bridge Robin asked if it was strong enough as he thought that it would barely hold the weight of the loaf let alone anything else. The Devil was scathing and told Robin to throw the loaf onto the bridge to prove that it was, indeed, strong enough. The dog eagerly ran after the loaf only to be killed by the Devil. Cleverly Robin had denied the Devil of a human soul and went back to the pub to finish his drinking.

Pont Aberglaslyn looking at the downstream side

PONT AR DDIBYN

Map: Ordnance Survey 1:25,000 Explorer series OL 23 Cadair Idris & Llyn Tegid
Grid reference: SH 761 178

Situated on Afon Clywedog the bridge is very close to the start of the famous and very pretty 'Torrent Walk' from Brithdir. It is also only 1½ miles downstream of Pont Gwanas. Pont ar Ddibyn has a single pointed arch with double arch rings and carries the B4416 over 'The Torrent'. The road is only 10 feet 8 inches or 3.29 metres wide, making it impossible for large truck, The 4 feet or 1.22 metres high parapets have recently been rebuilt during the improvements to the A470 a short distance away. It is a much later addition than other bridges on the Afon Clywedog and has been built of dressed stone.

The 'Torrent Walk' was designed and engineered by Thomas Payne who also designed the Cob, a raised embankment over the estuary at Porthmadog. He died in 1834 aged 73. There is a memorial plaque to him in St Mark's church in Brithdir. The church is well worth a visit. It is a grade 1 listed building, one of only a few in Wales.

It has been taken over by the Friends of Friendless Churches, a voluntary organisation formed in 1957 by Ivor Bulmer-Thomas to save churches and chapels of historic and architectural interest threatened by demolition or conversion. The church was built between 1885 and 1895 to the designs of Henry Wilson and is one of only a few Art Nouveau churches in Wales. The choir stalls are made from Spanish chestnut and are superbly carved with a hare, tortoise, squirrels, rabbits, an owl, a kingfisher and a dolphin. The architects dream was that 'the church should appear as if it had sprung out of the soil'.

Pont ar Ddibyn, looking upstream.

PONT AR DDYFI

Map: Ordnance Survey 1:25,000 Explorer series OL 23 Cadair Idris & Llyn Tegid
Grid reference: SH 744 019

This bridge spans Afon Dyfi very close to Machynlleth at the boundary of the Snowdonia National Park. It is marked as an antiquity on the OS map. The river also marks the boundary between Powys and Gwynedd. There was a crossing here as far back as the middle ages. In 1533 Geoffrey Hughes, a merchant from London left £6 13s and 4p (£6.67 in pre decimal money) in his will 'towardes the making of a bridge at the town of Mathanleth'. One was built but in 1681 at the Sessions ' Dyfi Bridge in the hundred of Mochunlleth was insufficient'. It was either that the bridge was not a solid one or the floods, that occur most years, took their toll is not known

Although it is known that the Romans crossed Afon Dyfi it may well have been nearer to their fort at Pennal. The present stone bridge was built in 1804 costing the princely sum of £250! It was described as fine bridge with five arches. The bridge piers are narrow and have a pilaster over each of the small cutwaters and a string course at road level. Although there is salmon in the river numbers have declined in recent years. Poaching at one time was a problem with, on occasion, dynamiting to stun the fish. The bridge is best viewed from the downstream side. At the beginning of 2020 it was announced that the bridge is to be replaced downstream of the current one which in effect will mean that Machynlleth will be bypassed. The bridge parapet is frequently damaged by trucks as they turn left to Aberdyfi or right into Machynlleth.

The history of Machynlleth goes back a long way in time. Copper mining took place within a mile of the town centre in the early Bronze Age some 2,750 years ago. The Romans came here and built a small fort at Pennal, 4 miles to the west on the way to Aberdyfi. There was also, supposedly, two look out stations above the town at Bryn y Gog and Wylfa. A Royal Charter was granted in 1291 by Edward 1 to the Lord of Powys at that time Owen de la Pole. The charter gave the right to hold a market every Wednesday for all time and to hold two fairs every year. To this day the Wednesday market still takes place and

remains very popular. The fairs also take place twice a year.

In 1404 Machynlleth became the seat for Owain Glyndŵr's Welsh Parliament having been crowned Prince of Wales before the leaders of Scotland, France and Spain that year. The town claims to be the 'ancient capital of Wales' although it never did receive any official recognition as such, whilst some argue that the town should be THE capital as it was the seat of the original parliament!

Below the clock tower there is what is known as Royal House where Dafydd Gam was imprisoned from 1404 to 1412 for attempting to assassinate Owain Glyndŵr. However, upon his release by Glyndŵr Dafydd fought alongside Henry V at the Battle of Agincourt and is immortalised in Shakespeare's play Henry V as one of the dead! Charles 1 is supposed to have stayed

1. & 2. Pont ar Ddyfi upstream side.

in the house in 1643 but no documentary evidence of this. In 1644 a battle during the Civil War took place near to the bridge between Oliver Cromwell's army commanded by Sir Thomas Myddelton and the Royalists. Many Royalist houses were burned down.

The first railway station in Machynlleth was on the narrow gauge line from Corris to Derwenlas for the transportation of slates from the quarries around Corris and Aberllefenni. At one time small boats were able to dock at Derwenlas. This line opened in 1859. The main line station was opened in 1863 upon the opening of the Newtown and Machynlleth railway. In 1864 the line was extended to Aberystwyth via Dyfi Junction. The current station at Machynlleth was built in 1905.

The clock tower in Machynlleth is a striking feature of the town!! The foundation stone was laid on the 15t July 1874. It was erected by the townspeople to celebrate the coming of age of Charles Stewart Vane-Tempest, Viscount Castlereagh the eldest son of the Earl of Vane and his wife. Another of their sons Lord Herbert Vane-Tempest lived in Y Plas at the southern end of town. He was the last person to live there and was,

unfortunately, killed in a train crash at Abermule on the 26th January 1921 along with 16 others. During World War II Y Plas became a military facility before being given to the town.

PONT AR EDEN

Map: 1:25,000 Ordnance Survey Explorer series OL 18 Harlech, Porthmadog & Bala/Y Bala
Grid reference: SH 727 248

A bridge spanning Afon Eden has been here since the early 18th century. The one seen here today is one constructed some 100 years later. It has a lovely single arch span, which, on still mornings the arch is perfectly mirrored in the pool below. The road it carries continues to a parking area from which a walk leads to the Gwynfynydd gold mine and Rhaeadr Mawddach, although an occasional truck lumbers up to the mine. The width of the carriageway is a mere 12 feet or 3.6 metres.

1. Pont ar Eden; 2. Pont ar Gonwy.

PONT AR GONWY

Map: Ordnance Survey 1:25,000 Explorer series OL 18 Harlech, Porthmadog & Bala/Y Bala
Grid reference: SH 778 446

This is one of the eighteen bridges that span Afon Conwy. It carries the B4407 across an area known as the Migneint. The bridge is very near to Llyn Cottage and the track leading to Llyn Conwy. The bridge is formed of three square lintel arches making it an unusual structure for a road. It is well worth visiting.

Llyn Conwy is the largest in this area. During the 1880's it was a renowned fishing lake. In June 1880 it was reported that 111 trout were caught over 2 days! Quite a prodigious figure. In those days the ground was heavily and 'professionally managed' for shooting and fishing.

One of the more 'interesting' managers employed by Lord Penrhyn was a chap called Andrew Foster who became the head keeper for him in 1874. He hailed from Scotland where no doubt he learned his skills. Poaching was rife even so and successive 'managers' tried everything to prevent it A technique known as 'otterboarding' was used by the poachers. Otterboarding used a pair of large, heavy square or rectangular plates or boards of metal or weighted wood attached to trawl lines on each side of a trawl net to maintain lateral spread during trawling. It was very efficient and commonly used by poachers in the Snowdonia lakes.

Nailed poles were floated and tied down with wire as well as being weighted down with rocks in an attempt to thwart the poachers. The fine for those days was a very hefty £1. 15s. 6d (£1.78). There were many other managing projects, such as transplanting lily roots from Llyn Serw on the opposite side of the road and the extermination of all the black-headed gulls from one of the three islands on the lake as they ate grouse eggs. Llyn Cottage was used as a base for night fishing by Lord Penrhyn's family and friends. The original Welsh name for the house was Corlan Muriau Gwynion.

Associated with the lake is a legend which said that the lake was once owned by the Knights of St. John of Jerusalem up until the dissolution of the monasteries in 1536. Finally, at the turn of the 19th century the housekeeper at Llyn Cottage, Anna Jane who lived in Swch, Penmachno set off from her home to go to work at the cottage. She was advised not to do so in view of the awful weather with snow falling. Sadly she died within sight of the cottage. There is the remains of a cottage on the south shore, now alas with a water covered floor. This was used also utilised as a night base for fishing.

> 1. *Pont ar Gonwy looking upstream;*
> 2. *Pont ar Ledr looking downstream.*

PONT AR LEDR

Map: Ordnance Survey 1:25,000 Explorer series OL 18 Harlech, Porthmadog & Bala/Y Bala
Grid reference: SH 796 541

Not named on the OS map. As the name suggests this pretty bridge spans Afon Lledr just before its confluence with Afon Conwy. Originally a bridge was built on this site in the 1500's by Hywel Saer-maen prior to him building Pont-y-pair in Betws-y-coed. The bridge seen today, however, dates from circa 1700. It has two arches, a main one spanning the river and a smaller one close to the main road absorbs floodwater. The minor road the bridge carries has a width of only 11 feet or 3.3 metres. The bridge is a wonderful sight in autumn when the leaves on the surrounding trees are blessed with a shade of wonderful orange. The water tumbles noisily through boulders in its final few yards voyage to Afon Conwy. The Edwardians must have been impressed with this bridge as they produced coloured postcards and the diligent can still find them today.

PONT BREN
(Beddgelert Bridge)

Map: Ordnance Survey 1:25,000 Explorer series OL 17 Snowdon/Yr Wyddfa
Grid reference: SH 590 481

Situated in the centre of the village it spans Afon Colwyn just upstream of its confluence with Afon Glaslyn. More than likely a bridge existed here before The Dissolution of the Monasteries in March 1536. The bridge would have allowed access to the Augustinian Priory on the northern side of the river. In 1623 the bridge was repaired and again in 1778. The big flood of 1799 swept away much of the bridge. Repair work ensued and it was also widened between 1802 and 1811when a toll was levied. further repairs took place around 1890 and again in 1906.

Pont Bren has three segmented arches and constructed from rubble and rises from a cobbled plinth raft that projects beyond the bridge itself. The voussoirs are roughly dressed and narrow stones form projecting arch rings. The central arch allows the main flow of Afon Colwyn to pass below. There is slightly smaller arch to the north whilst the small southern one acts as a flood arch. The carriageway is humped in the centre and on each side is a recess or refuge above the cutwaters. The coping or capping stones are long slate slabs resting on the rubble parapets.

Interestingly there are slate milestones on the downstream internal wall of the parapet at the northern end. they are possibly late 19th or early 20th century in origin. The left hand one is inscribed To Penygwryd 7; To Llanberis 13; To Capel Cuirig is an indistinct number. The right hand milestone is inscribed To Portmadoc 7½. On the north side splayed parapets continue beyond the bridge approach as low rubble walls running parallel to the river on both sides and extend 100 metres or 330 feet. They have a roadside height of .6 metre or 2 feet. To the south the roadside parapet is 1m or 3 feet and extends a similar distance. A feature in the downstream angle is a squinch. A Squinch is a small arch, or sometimes a lintel, stretching across an angle.

Beddgelert, Gelert's Grave, is one of the most beautiful villages in North Wales

1. Pont Bren Beddgelert;
2. Pont Bren, Beddgelert, looking upstream.

and is reputed to be named after the legendary hound Gelert. However, the village possibly came by this name after an early Christian missionary and leader called Celert, or Cilert, settled here in the 8th century. The earliest record of Beddgelert appears in 1258 when it was recorded as Bekelert, whilst in 1269 it is recorded as Bedkelerd. The Church of St Mary was originally the chapel of a Benedictine monastery and parts of the building date back to the 12th century. Standing at the confluence of Afon Glaslyn and Afon Colwyn the village is situated in a pretty valley. Many of the houses and hotels are built from the local dark stone. Moel Hebog is the dominant mountain to the west of the village. Caernarfon is 13 miles to the north and Porthmadog 8 miles to the south. It is also within easy reach of Betws-y-coed 14 miles away.

The central point of the village is the old, arched bridge just upstream of the confluence. The original bridge was destroyed by a catastrophic flood in 1799 and was badly damaged again in the early part of the 20th century. Beddgelert was once a thriving port before The Cob at Porthmadog was built by William Maddocks in 1811. Ships docked at the village of Aberglaslyn (Aber), a small port just below Pont Aberglaslyn, where the tidal river ended.

Alfred Bestall M.B.E. wrote and illustrated some of his Rupert Bear stories when he lived in the village. His cottage is situated at the foot of Mynydd Sygun. George Borrow visited the village in 1854 on his journey through Wales and is mentioned in his wonderful book, *Wild Wales*, published in 1862. He called the Gelert valley "a wondrous valley - rivalling for grandeur and beauty any vale either in the Alps or Pyrenees".

Rupert Bear was created by the English artist Mary Tourtel. The first comic strip first appeared in the Daily Express on 8 November 1920. In 1935 the Rupert stories were taken over by Alfred Edmeades Bestall M.B.E. an artist and storyteller. Born in Mandalay, Burma on 14th December 1892, he died on the 15th January 1986. Alfred lived in the house from 1956 to 1986. His first story was published on the 28th June 1935 and the last on the 22nd July 1965 although he still did covers for Rupert Annuals until 1973. The character Rupert Bear lives with his parents in a house in Nutwood, a fictional idyllic English village. He is depicted wearing a red sweater and bright yellow checked trousers, with matching yellow scarf. Usually seen as a white bear he was originally brown and was made white to save on printing costs.

The majority of the other characters in the series are also anthropomorphic animals (animals with humanoid forms). Regardless of species they are all drawn roughly the same size as Rupert referring to them as his "chums" or "pals". His best friend was Bill Badger. Others were an elephant (Edward Trunk), a mouse (Willie), Pong-Ping the Pekingese, Algy Pug, Podgy Pig, Bingo the Brainy Pup, Freddie and Ferdy Fox, and finally Ming the dragon.

Rupert was helped on many of his adventures by the kindly Wise Old Goat who also lives in Nutwood. The few main human characters in the stories were the Professor (who lives in a castle with his servant), Tiger Lily (a Chinese girl), and her father 'The Conjuror'. Perhaps Alfred's most famous drawing was 'The Frog's Chorus'. This inspired the cartoon video 'The Frog Song' composed by Sir Paul McCartney.

PONT CARREG ARW

Map: Ordnance Survey 1:25,000 Explorer series OL 18 Harlech, Porthmadog & Bala/Y Bala
Grid reference: SH 732 219

This is a modern construction but is included to give an example of a suspension bridge. It spans Afon Mawddach 1¾ miles north of Llanelltyd. It is difficult to view this bridge but it can be seen from the minor road on the east side of Afon Mawddach. It is privately owned.

Pont Carreg Arw.

PONT CARREG HYLLDREM

Map: Ordnance Survey 1:25,000 Explorer series OL 18 Harlech, Porthmadog & Bala/Y Bala

Grid reference: SH 615 431

This pretty bridge spans Afon Croesor once the river reaches the valley floor after tumbling down many waterfalls and cataracts from Cwm Croesor. There are great views of Cnicht and the Moelwynion from a lay-by near the bridge. The bridge carries the A4085 from Penrhyndeudraeth to Aberglaslyn. From the lay-by a crag above the road can be discerned. It is called Carreg Hylldrem and is home to many very steep and difficult rock climbs.

PONT CEDRIS

Map: Ordnance Survey 1:25,000 Explorer series OL 23 Cadair Idris & Llyn Tegid
Grid reference: SH 692 081

Carrying the B4405 Pont Cedris spans the Afon Dysynni which emanates from Llyn Mwyngul (Talyllyn), itself fed by numerous mountain streams, to flow down the Dysynni Valley. It is an unusual bridge as the arches are of different lengths. This may well have been because of the nature of the valley floor being composed of sediments and not being able to find a solid foundation for the arches. These are low with the smallest almost horizontal. One square flood opening completes the structure. There were two at one time but one is no longer visible as it is silted up. The construction is very similar to Pont ar Ddyfi at Machynlleth being built from slate slabs. There is also a string course. A small mark possibly the mason's which can be interpreted as a trowel and a hammer. The bridge was built

somewhere around the early 19th century although at one time the date 1865 was visible but cannot be seen nowadays. The width of the road was originally 13 feet or 4 metres but was widened on the downstream side in the winter of 1998/99. The parapets are 3 feet 3 inches or 1 metre high.

1. *Pont Carreg Hylldrem;*
2. *Pont Cedris looking downstream.*

PONT CYFYNG

Map: Ordnance Survey 1:25,000 Explorer series OL 17 Snowdon/Yr Wyddfa
Grid reference: SH 734 571

Spanning Afon Llugwy in Capel Curig this has great views of the Cyfyng waterfalls below. Only a few metres from the A5 it is easily seen from it. It is a narrow bridge being only 12 feet or 3.6 metres wide and was built in 1800 when the A5 was being constructed. The span is 34 feet or 10.4 metres and is crossed at the start of the walk up Moel Siabod 2,861 feet or 872 metres.

PONT DOLBENMAEN

Map: Ordnance Survey 1:25,000 Explorer series OL 254 Lleyn Peninsula East/Pen Llŷn Ardal Ddwyreiniol
Grid reference: SH 507 429

Spanning the Afon Dwyfor the original bridge is now almost hidden from view by the new one carrying the A487. Nowadays the only traffic it sees is from walkers. A ford once existed here but the old bridge dates from the late 18th century. The bridge comprises a segmental arch of flush rubble voussoirs on the north side whilst on the south it is of packed slate set back below a regulating course. The spandrels are flush with the parapet. This is topped with coping stones placed edge. The top of the arch is 11 feet or 3.35 metres above normal water level. The road is 12½ feet or 3.8 metres between the parapets. To the west a causeway continues across a narrow valley having three square topped flood openings.

1. *Pont Cyfyng, looking upstream.;*
2. *Pont Dolbenmaen, looking downstream.*

Dolbenmaen, literally means *'meadow at head of rock'*. Marking the end of Cwm Pennant Dolbenmaen was the administrative centre, *maerdref*, in Eifionydd until 1239. The community includes the villages of Bryncir, Cenin, Garn-dolben-maen, Golan, Llanfihangel-y-pennant, Penmorfa, Pentrefelin, and the hamlet of Prenteg. A castle motte is located to the south of the village which is thought to have been the residence of Llywelyn the Great until the 1230s, when the court moved to a motte and bailey castle at Criccieth. The castle guarded a ford on Afon Dwyfor which may have been on Pen Llystyn (Tremadog) to Segontium (Caernarfon) Roman road. The parish church of St Mary's is a grade II listed building.

The castle mound is 118 feet or 36 metres in diameter and some 20 feet or 6 metres high and can be clearly seen from the road despite the trees. On the flat top there is a vague hint of the long vanished stone buildings. Unfortunately it is situated on private land and impossible to visit. A substantial ditch survives on the west, but on the other sides, the base has been damaged by later walls. The mound is worth a look because the grouping of church, castle and manor house, Plas Dolbenmaen, is both attractive and unusual for Wales, as closely knit villages such as this are rare. A village of bondmen would have been attached to the court to work the Lord's fields, hence the tight cluster of houses around it.

PONT DOLGEFEILIAU

Map: Ordnance Survey 1:25,000 Explorer series OL 18 Harlech, Porthmadog & Bala/Y Bala
Grid reference: SH 721 269

Spanning Afon Eden this bridge once carried the A470, the trunk road through Wales from Cardiff to Llandudno. The new road is a very short distance to the west. The bridge can easily be reached from the Coed y Brenin Visitor and Mountain Bike Centre by a short gentle walk. The bridge was bypassed because the road was carried at right angles over it and caused huge problems for drivers of long vehicles.

Pont Dolgefeiliau, looking upstream.

PONT DÔL-Y-MOCH (road bridge)

Map: Ordnance Survey 1:25,000 Explorer series OL 18 Harlech, Porthmadog & Bala/Y Bala
Grid reference: SH 684 416

Carrying the narrow minor road up the Vale of Ffestiniog this attractive looking bridge spans Afon Goedol, a few metres before its confluence with the Afon Cynfal and when these rivers have combined they continue as the Afon Dwyryd. Marked as an antiquity on the OS map it was built around 1790. There are four recesses on top of the bridge with two having seats. Not a bad place to view the river as the road is very quiet indeed as it seems to only serve the farms along it. The parapet is unusually low at under 2 feet or 60 centimetres whilst the width of the road is only 8 feet or 2.4 metres. It is possibly the best well preserved of ancient bridges of its type in Snowdonia.

1. *Pont Dôl-y-moch (Afon Goedol) Looking upstream. Note the cutwaters on the downstream side;* 2. *Pont Dôl-y-moch Looking upstream;* 3. *Pont Dôl-y-moch Recess on the top of an upstream cutwater.*

PONT DÔL-Y-MOCH (track bridge)

Map: Ordnance Survey 1:25,000 Explorer series OL 18 Harlech, Porthmadog & Bala/Y Bala
Grid reference: SH 685 415

This old bridge can easily be seen from the narrow road running up the Vale of Ffestiniog 100yards or 100 metres after crossing the road bridge mentioned above. It spans Afon Cynfal. However, it is in a sad state of repair. The bridge has also been known as Pont Dolrhiwfelen and carried the ancient and important route from Gellilydan to Plas Dôl-y-moch. Although looking much older than the road bridge time has not been kind to it as it was built around the same time. The track over the bridge has a width of 15 feet or 4.6 metres. It is now grassed over and is seldom used.

1. *Pont Dôl-y-moch (Afon Cynfal) looking upstream; 2. Pont Dôl-y-moch, old bridge seen from the downstream side; 3. Pont Dysynni looking down to this old bridge from the new road bridge.*

PONT DYSYNNI

Map: Ordnance Survey 1:25,000 Explorer series OL 18 Harlech, Porthmadog & Bala/Y Bala
Grid reference: SH 599 038

Spanning the now tidal Afon Dysynni the old bridge, built from local stone rubble and slightly humped, once carried the A493 and has four arches. It has been replaced by an unattractive modern bridge that now carries this road. The old bridge dates from the late 18th century being built after the passing of the Turnpike Act in 1784. The arches each have a span of 21 feet or 6.3 metres of squared voussoirs. They are 6 feet or 1.8 metres above water level. The parapet has stone coping flags. The piers for the bridge are set on starlings each with a 120 degree cutwater to each side. The road is 12 feet 6 inches wide or 3.8 metres sat between the parapets of 2 feet 8 inches or .85 metre high. The plan view shows the bridge has a slight 'S' curve. Interestingly an iron plate on each side of the parapet, made by Isaac of Portmadoc, indicates that vehicular traffic is banned from crossing due to the bridge being weak!

PONT FADOG

Map: Ordnance Survey 1: 25,000 Explorer series OL18 Harech, Porthmadog & Bala/ Y Bala
Grid reference: SH 607 225

This Grade II listed bridge is situated on the old drovers' route from Bwlch y Rhiwgyr to Bont-ddu and Dolgellau. It spans Afon Ysgethin and is dated 1762 although the route had been improved in 1760.

The bridge construction is of rubble masonry with a single arch with 2 feet 3 inches or 69 centimetres low parapet walls that are covered by stone slab coping stones. The road width on the bridge is 7 feet or 2.13 metres. In the middle of the downstream parapet the upright stone tablet has the following fading inscriptions - W V 1762 H E SAER. The Welsh word saer refers to a builder or carpenter.

The W V initials on the large upright stone in the middle of the downstream side of the bridge are of William Vaughan from Cors y Gedol. He paid for the improvements to the existing bridge whilst the other initials, H E., relate to H. Edward the mason commissioned to carry out the work.

Situated above and between Dyffryn Ardudwy and Tal-y-bont the best way to reach this bridge is by following the path from Tal-y-bont alongside the Afon Ysgethin up to the end of the tarmac road by a house, Llety Lloegr which literally means 'lodging house on the road to England' a mark of the drovers' links with this track. The bridge is down to the right. A return can be made along the road passing a fine Neolithic burial chamber dating back 5,000 years and the rambling Cors y Gedol Hall en route back into Talybont.

Cors y Gedol literally means the 'bog of hospitality'. This may sound strange nowadays but several centuries ago the surrounding area was very marshy and may account for the rather odd title. Cors y gedol was the home of the Vaughan family until 1791 by which time the family had died out. They were one of the main families in the area and were descendents of Osborn Fitzgerald an Irishman who settled here in the 13th century. The Vaughan's were well respected and prominent in Meirioneth affairs serving as MPs, High Sheriffs and Magistrates. The Mostyn's, another aristocratic family, having been passed the estate, lived here until 1860 after the Vaughan's. The present building dates back to 1576 but has undergone much alteration and additions since then.

Talybont was, many years ago, a collecting point for animals before their crossing of the Rhinogydd to markets in England. Drovers used to drive some 400 animals over these bleak mountains along these now ancient track-ways to market. Animals were shod with metal shoes, pigs wore woollen socks with leather soles, what a sight that must have been, and geese were given a layer a hardened tar and sand to protect their feet during the rough journey. Today these track-ways can still be seen and are a part of what I think is the most unspoilt National Nature Reserve in Wales.

PONT FAWR

Map: Ordnance Survey 1:25,000 Explorer series OL 17 Snowdon/Yr Wyddfa
Grid reference: SH 798 614

Although not actually in the National Park I have included it for its fine architectural form and the OS map reveals it is classed as an antiquity. The design of Pont Fawr is attributed to Inigo Jones in 1636. Sir Richard Wynn, from the nearby Castell Gwydir, was acting as the Treasurer to the Queen and would have paid Jones and his Master Mason Nicholas Stone. The design

Pont Fawr, Llanrwst, looking downstream.

possibly stems from a similar one based on one by Palladio. Pont Fawr has the same dimensions and form as this. There are three segmental arches. The main and middle one is 60 feet or 18.2 metres wide and 24 feet or 7.3 metres high whilst the two outer ones are each have a span of 48 feet or 15 metres. The width of the roadway is 13 feet or 4 metres wide. Cutwaters on each side extend upwards to create refuges in the parapet. Prior to 1636 a bridge spanned Afon Conwy but was deemed unsafe in 1627.

The arch on the side furthest from the town is known to have been built in 1675 and again in 1703. It is thought that the central arch collapsed on the opening day due to the keystone being fitted upside down! This was probably due to the fact that the workmen were drunk whilst working on the construction. Mead was a part of their building contract. The workmen employed to rebuild the bridge were instructed to drink nothing stronger than buttermilk. For some years after completion the bridge became known as Pont Llaeth Enwyn *buttermilk bridge*.

A stone on the inner side of the south parapet and above the arch has the initials TR. It was built from local millstone grit (gritstone) and slate rubble. The coping stones are steeply chamfered and connected by iron cramps. Above the apex of the central arch the south parapet has a stone relief of the Stuart Arms with the initials CR. Below this is the date 1636. The Arms are set inside a frame with superimposed fluted columns which support floral entablature and ogee cresting. The sundial above was erected for the bridge's tercentenary.

The north parapet has the Prince of Wales feathers splaying out from a crown which has the initials CP. The inside wall of the parapet has carriage stones that protect the masonry. Once motor vehicles started using the bridge and prior to the installation of traffic lights the bridge had taken on another name, Pont y Rhegi or in English '*the swearing bridge*' due to the many near misses and the lack of a courteous attitude resulting in road rage.

PONT FELIN-Y-FFRIDD

Map: Ordnance Survey 1:25,000 Explorer series OL 23 Cadair Idris & Llyn Tegid
Grid reference: SH 751 024
Also known as Pont Glan Gwynedd

This three arch bridge spans the Afon Dulais close to its confluence with the Afon Dyfi not far from Machynlleth on the Snowdonia National Park boundary. The arches are of different sizes and span 90 feet or 27.4 metres. The bridge was probably built early in the 19th century on the site of an old ford or wooden bridge and possibly around the same time as the present Pont ar Ddyfi. Built from poor quality slate and showing signs of deterioration and is held together with huge, long steel bolts passing through the faces. Only one of the original cutwaters remains as the others have been patched with concrete. The bridge nowadays has a width of 15 feet or 4.6 metres and although there are no visible signs it may have been widened at some stage.

Pont Felin-y-ffridd looking upstream in high water.

PONT GETHIN

Map: Ordnance Survey 1:25,000 Explorer series OL 18 Harlech, Porthmadog & Bala/Y Bala
Grid reference: SH 525 451

This is an imposing viaduct spanning the A470 main road through Wales from Cardiff to Llandudno. It carries the railway line from Blaenau Ffestiniog to Llandudno and is situated close to Pont Lledr and Beaver Bridge and Betws-y-coed. This impressive structure was the work of Owen Gethin Jones a poet, author and historian. He was born in 1816 in the parish of Penmachno. He became a Master Craftsman, a stone mason and talented writer. He designed the viaduct by himself as well as constructing it with a small number of workmen. Gethin did most of the detailed stonework himself. One of his other achievements was building the railway station in Betws-y-coed regarded as one of the finest in Wales in the day. He died in 1883.

1. Pont Gethin, view from the road;
2. Pont Gethin. from the Afon Lledr.

PONT GWANAS

Map: Ordnance Survey 1:25,000 Explorer series OL 23 Cadair Idris & Llyn Tegid
Grid reference: SH 768 167

The original Pont Gwanas , described here, was bypassed in 1930 during improvements to the A470. The overgrown roadway is 15 feet 5 inches or 4.72 metres wide. This bridge and the new one span Afon Clywedog. On the upstream side the bridge has a central cutwater between the two segmented arches with single arch rings. On the downstream side there is only a pilaster and double arch rings. The parapet is 2 feet 8 inches or 81 centimetres high with flat copings on top. On the true right on the upstream side there is a stone built wall. It is an attractive bridge and is easily accessed from the nearby lay-by.

The new bridge, a little distance upstream, was probably the last traditionally built stone bridge to be constructed. There is a slate inscription on the downstream parapet - Merionethshire County Council, Gwanas Bridge, opened by the Right Honourable Herbert Morrison Esq. M. P. Minister of Transport 26 June 1930.

1. Pont Gwanas looking downstream;
2. Pont Gwanas looking upstream.

PONT GWYNFYNYDD

Map: Ordnance Survey 1:25,000 Explorer series OL 18 Harlech, Porthmadog & Bala/Y Bala
Grid reference: SH 729 278

Although of no great vintage this bridge spanning the Afon Mawddach in Coed y Brenin is included to show that bridges can be constructed to look like the originals. The present bridge replaces one of 18th century vintage when it was swept away in the floods of 2001. Although a footbridge replaced it a new masonry arch bridge that would carry forestry traffic was needed. A company called Reinforced Earth designed and supplied single piece arch units and TerraTrel bridge spandrel walls to form the bridge structure. Precast construction was important to minimise the risk of polluting the river. Being in the Snowdonia national Park it was important that no concrete was visible.

Bespoke precast concrete parapet units were also supplied by Reinforced Earth Company. The structure is clad with locally quarried stone to give a traditional appearance to this modern high performance structure. The bridge won the Constructing Excellence Award for Innovation in 2007.

A walk is needed to see this bridge. It starts from the car park at Tyddyn Gwladys and follows firstly the tarmac road until it ends and then a track which passes close to Pistyll Cain, Gwynfynydd Gold Mine and Rhaeadr Mwaddach to cross the bridge and then down the other side of the river to a footbridge leading back to the car park.

Although gold was discovered in 1863 it was not until 1887 that any real profit was made. It was a laborious job with a working day both hard and long. In 1888 Hugh Pugh from Dolgellau started work here. He wrote diaries which gave a fascinating insight into the methods and conditions prevailing at that time. Some 200 men were employed with many of them boys under 15. They worked a 10 hour shift!

Many of the miners lived in barracks at the mine although some took up lodgings in nearby farms whilst others had long walks from their homes each day whatever the weather. The 'white collar' people in charge lodged away from the miners in a separate boarding house. Hugh for

Pont Gwynfynydd looking upstream.

example walked 8½ miles. He told of meeting at a bridge with others at 03.00 to start work at 07.00 with their 'wallets'. In one end would be a big homemade loaf whilst at the other would be rations.

For those staying at the mine a horse and cart travelled to Dolgellau each day for supplies and once a week bread and other groceries were delivered to the mine. However, the menu on offer seemed somewhat monotonous. One miner reflected his view as follows -

'Rabbits young, rabbits old,
Rabbits hot, rabbits cold,
Rabbits tender, rabbits tough,
Thank the Lord, we had enough'

There was no entertainment although sing songs were usually held on Friday nights with a concert once a month. One of the mine managers opened a reading room and started a Bible class. Wages were poor and in 1900 a miner was paid 3 shillings and 6 pence (18 new pence) and 1 shilling and 6 pence (8 pence) for a boy whilst a poor donkey only received 1 shilling and a penny (6 pence)!

The Dolgellau Gold Belt heralded the 'Welsh Gold Rush' in 1860 with many companies prospecting in the area. The Ty'n Groes Hotel (then known as Thornton's Hotel) became the focal and meeting place for the miners. The gold belt extends for about 20 miles and 20 mines were operational at the peak of production at that time but many were tiny affairs with few miners. The rock dates back to the Cambrian period some 550 million years ago.

The first 'rush' was over by 1865 and for the next 20 years or so intermittent concerns continued until 1887 when William Pritchard Morgan owned the mine. He was eventually dubbed the 'Welsh Gold King'. Reputedly he made two fortunes here. The new discoveries were better organised, better equipped and with better finance. During this period 30 mines became operational but again many were small undertakings being little more than mere scratchings on the surface. Pritchard discovered a lode that became known as the Chidlaw Lode. It was one of several but this was the richest. Gold ore is considered rich if it contains 1 ounce of gold per ton of rock! 8,745 ounces of gold were produced from 3,844 tons of rock. This was more than double the amount of richness with 2.27 ounces of gold per ton. Pritchard once boasted that in two weeks he produced 2 stone more gold than his weight!

In 1894 Pritchard discovered another lode that produced 10,000 ounce over a 2 year period. He sold the mine in 1900 but bought it back again in 1913 but with limited success this time and finally the mine closed in 1916. By comparison the amount of gold produced here between 1863 and 1916 would amount to £20 million.

Traditionally gold produced in Wales was used for wedding rings for the Royal Family. The ingot of gold presented to Queen Victoria was exhausted by 1960. In 1986 a kilogram of 99% pure gold ingot was presented to Queen Elizabeth to commemorate her 60th birthday and a smaller one given to the Duke of York.

Gold was extracted from the ore in the Gwynfynydd Mills. These were powered by a waterwheel and turbines. The ore was tipped onto screens then fed into stonebreakers before being crushed by stamp mills then being washed over copper plates covered with amalgam that picked up the gold. Grinding Pans, known as 'Britten Pans' were used to recover the visible gold from the higher grade ore. Smelting was also carried out here. Hugh Pugh who was mentioned above became a foreman and in one of his diaries he records that the Britten Pans worked from Sunday midnight through to Saturday midnight and operated by two men working 12 hour shifts!

Pont Gyfyng road bridge looking downstream, Cwm Pennant.

PONT GYFYNG (Road bridge)

Map: Ordnance Survey 1:25,000 Explorer series OL 254 Lleyn Peninsula East/Pen Llŷn Ardal Ddwyreiniol
Grid reference: SH 526 449

Spanning Afon Dwyfor this single arch bridge carries the narrow minor road up Cwm Pennant and is found very close to Llanfihangel-y-Pennant. It is best seen from the upstream side. There is a wider section of road having crossed over immediately after where it is possible to park a couple of cars easily without blocking the road. The road width is 3.65 metres. Each parapet is 71 centimetres high. On the true left there are three flood arches. There is a single cutwater on the upstream side.

PONT GYFYNG

On the track leading to Moelfre slate quarry

Map: Ordnance Survey 1:25,000 Explorer series OL 254 Lleyn Peninsula East/Pen Llŷn Ardal Ddwyeiniol
Grid reference: SH 526 449

This bridge over Afon Dwyfor probably dates from the mid 1860's and situated close to the nearby hamlet of Llanfihangel y Pennant in Cwm Pennant. It was constructed to facilitate access to the Moelfre slate quarry. The construction from local rubble comprises two segmental arches spanning 18 feet or 5.6 metres on to a central rough stone cutwater. Each arch of shaped rubble voussoirs rise 8½ feet or 2.6 metres and are set flush with the spandrels. The track is 9 feet or 2.83 metres wide with 19 inches or 48 centimetres high parapets.

1.& 2. Pont Gyfyng track bridge looking upstream, Cwm Pennant.

PONT HELYGOG

Map: Ordnance Survey 1:25,000 Explorer series OL 23 Cadair Idris & Llyn Tegid
Grid reference: SH 792 196

Spanning the Nant Helygog close to Brithdir this is an ancient single span bridge and may possibly date back to Roman times as it is situated close to the site of a small Roman fort. The boulder built foundations and piers are much wider than the present bridge suggesting the bridge was, at one time, much wider. Of rubble construction with a simple rustic arch the 4 feet or 1.22 metres high parapet on the right or south side of the bridge is almost 'S' shaped and has no copings. The track is only 7 feet wide or 2.13 metres wide. It seems that there has always been a bridge here rather than a ford and has been repaired several times over the centuries although width of the rough track has shrunk from its original. In 1830 it was simply called 'the old bridge'. The parapets were repaired at that time.

1. *Pont Helygog looking upstream;*
2. *Pont Helygog looking downstream.*

PONT LLAM YR EWIG

Map: Ordnance Survey 1:25,000 Explorer series OL 18 Harlech, Porthmadog & Bala/Y Bala
Grid reference: SH 742 226

Not marked on the OS map. Translated Pont Llam yr Ewig is the '*bridge of the hind's leap*'. Local folklore says that a fairy baby was exchanged for a local farmer's child! The curved bridge spans the impressive Afon Babi. There is a small car park close by for the less able. For others the bridge can be accessed by starting from the Glasdir Natural Resources Wales car park and walking the Glasdir copper mine trail.

Glasdir mine was one of the most extensive mines in the Dolgellau area. It was first opened around 1852 as a quarry. Between 1872 and 1913 some 13,077 tons of dressed copper left the mine. In 1907 the mine was fortunate to have a mill using the Elmore Flotation Process. The process was brought here by Stanley Elmore the owner of the mine had previously constructed the process at the Sygun Copper Mine but when the mine stopped

Pont Llam yr Ewig looking downstream.

working he transferred all the equipment to Glasdir. The mine finally closed in 1915. In terms of precious metals the mine produced 8,275 ounces of silver and 735 ounces of gold between 1872 and 1915.

The flotation process entails using the waste material and water. This waste usually has some 1% - 2% of copper ore and is crushed. Water is then added and fed into a ball mill which is a rotating drum with steel balls that crush the ore into a fine powder to form slurry. This is then fed into a rake classifier when it comes out of the mill and then into flotation cells. Any particles that are too large are returned to the mill. Air is injected into the flotation cells where foaming agents are added. This creates froth and copper particles, because of their light weight, become a part of this froth. Heavier particles such as iron sink. The mixture of copper and froth containing around 20% - 40% copper continues for further processing to extract the copper itself.

PONT LLAERON

Map: Ordnance Survey 1:25,000 Explorer series OL 23 Cadair Idris & Llyn Tegid
Grid reference: SH 701 049

This very ancient and very pretty single arch pack horse bridge has been nicknamed 'the bridge to nowhere'. Faint paths lead to and from it. It is a pretty bridge set among wet ground. It may well have been on the St David's to Bangor route in ancient times as well as and likely, a crossing on Cadfan's Way. This is an old route that started in Machynlleth and went via Bryn Eglwys to Abergynolwyn and thence to Tywyn. It is also purported to be part of a Pilgrim route from Machynlleth to Ynys Enlli (Bardsey Island). Unfortunately all the parapet stones have been removed. This is probably due to people seeking pleasure in vandalising ancient structures. The width of the original bridge was only 6 feet or 1.8 metres when the parapets existed but now it is 8 feet or 2.4 metres and the bridge has a length of 30 feet or 9.1 metres. Although records exist that the bridge had been

Pont Llaeron looking upstream.

at one point, a fine waterfall plunging into a pit although a little bush whacking is required to find it! Here things become more difficult and interconnecting paths followed to reach the bridge.

Bryn Eglwys was the largest quarry south of Blaenau Ffestiniog and the workings and spoil spread over a wide area. Initially work started as several surface scratchings in the early 1800's on farmland were developed underground at both Cantrebedd and Bryneglwys farms in the 1840's.

repaired in 1756 it almost certainly existed well before then.

Although walking is necessary to reach this bridge an easy start can be made by taking the train journey from Tywyn to Nant Gwernol by walking up from Abergynolwyn. Walking from either of these two points is on good forest roads and clearly marked paths that pass through the Bryn Eglwys slate mine workings. There are wind up radios at several points telling the story of the area. A number of ruins can be found herewith,

Due to the lack of cotton arriving from America during the Civil War and their mills idle Lancashire men came down and worked in the quarry. They also built the Talyllyn Railway which opened in 1866 and whilst not going directly to a dock it did go to an interchange of the Cambrian Railway. Prior to this slate was taken out by packhorse to Pennal and then onto the dock at Aberdyfi. John Pugh of Penegoes, a village not far from Machynlleth, started extracting slate from Bryn Eglwys in 1844.

PONT LLAN

Map: Ordnance Survey 1:25,000
Explorer series OL 18 Harlech,
Porthmadog & Bala/Y Bala
Grid reference: 791 505

Not marked on the OS map. This bridge carries the B4406 in Penmachno before it continues to its end at Cwm Penmachno. It is a grand bridge of some antiquity. The original bridge was swept away during the great storm of 1779. An inscription on the upstream parapet indicates that it was built by I Hughes and Harry Parry from 'Garnarvon' (note the old spelling of Caernarfon) in 1785. Another inscription on the parapet coping stone reads -

> Pont isel drafel ar dro – pont lydan
> I wladwyr drafaelio
> Pont a fydd mewn pant tra fo
> Pont ar ochor Pen Tre fachno

Translated as follows:-

A low bridge to travel along its curve;
A wide bridge for country folk to use;
A bridge that will stand in a hollow
While a bridge will ever be by the village of Machno.

Pont Llan, view from the upstream side.

PONT LLANELLTYD

Map: Ordnance Survey 1:25,000 Explorer series OL 23 Cadair Idris & Llyn Tegid
Grid reference: SH 717 193
Not marked on the OS map.

Not named on the OS 1;25,000 map. This bridge dates back to the middle of the 18th century and consists of five arches spanning Afon Mawddach. There are also flood overflow culverts on the southern bank. The bridge parapets are covered with capstones. The construction is typical for the times in Wales as the arches are wide and shallow. Now used as a footpath the bridge seems unaltered since it was built. It has a slight rise in the centre. A car park at the southern makes for easy access and is popular as a picnic site as well as with fishermen although a permit is required.

On the reverse of the stone is another inscription having the initials of JWMO IWE with a date of AD 1903. The stone also has the faint impression of two men with pipes that are said to be the builders of the bridge. The length of the bridge is 197 feet or 60 metres. It has five arches with the two main ones having a cutwater between them on the upstream side spanning the river. There are three flood arches to the west. The arches are elliptical with thin voussoirs. The parapet is 3 feet or 1 metre high.

1. Pont Llan. The inscription on top of an upstream parapet coping; 2. Pont Llan. The inscription on the face of a coping on the upstream side; 3. Pont Llanelltyd downstream side; 4. Pont Llanelltyd looking upstream.

PONT MAENTWROG

Map: Ordnance Survey 1:25,000 Explorer series OL 18 Harlech, Porthmadog & Bala/Y Bala
Grid reference: SH 664 407

No definite date has been credited to Pont Maentwrog but is loosely dated to the 1780's. Pont Maentwrog spans Afon Dwyryd at the northern end of the village of Maentwrog. The bridge has three quite shallow stone arches surmounted by stone parapets. At one time the bridge carried the A487 but being narrow traffic could have come to a standstill unless traffic lights were installed to ease this problem. Only the southern arch crosses flowing water whilst the others would have water flowing below them in times of heavy rainfall. The river is tidal up to a point a couple of hundred metres away. The two substantial piers stand in the riverbed and have large cutwaters on each side that taper somewhat towards the top. The bridge may have been reconstructed in the past due to the stonework above the arches being a slightly different colour.

1. Pont Maentwrog looking downstream; 2. Pont Maentwrog looking upstream; 3. Pont Maentwrog old mile post by side of bridge.

PONT MALLWYD

Map: Ordnance Survey 1:25,000 Explorer series OL 23 Cadair Idris & Llyn Tegid
Grid reference: SH 857 122

The bridge spans Afon Dyfi in a single arch at one of the narrowest but prettiest points of the river in the gorge below the tiny hamlet of Mallwyd. Bridge building here has a chequered history and difficult to determine. After much discussion it has been accepted that the bridge seen today was built at the turn of the 18th century. The width of the road between the 3 feet 4 inches or 1.02 metres high parapet is 8 feet 3 inches or 2.52 metres. Interestingly the slate coping stones are chamfered. Two other bridges had been built close by over

Pont Mallwyd looking downstream.

Afon Dyfi and another over the Afon Cleifion between 1633 and 1637. A bridge was built here in 1633 from timber resting on stone pillars. Another bridge called Ryfygan built at the same place was swept away in 1574! The bridge that replaced this was also swept away in 1614. The next bridge lasted only a year. Another was built at a different site further down the gorge but it too was swept away in 1632.

This appears to have been an important crossing as it was on the main route from Welshpool to Machynlleth. It is obvious bridges have been in existence here since medieval times. The present bridge has no record of who constructed it and the earliest reference is from 1808 when Richard Colt Hoare mentions it in his diaries stating that 'Crossed the Dovey near Mallwyd over a picturesque bridge, and the only one in a long distance between this place and Machynlleth'. Dovey is the Anglicised name for the Afon Dyfi.

Catastrophic flooding has occurred many times and in 1964 two bridges downstream were swept away and this bridge became the only crossing in twelve miles. Traffic across this bridge was light but included trucks and farm machinery. A new bridge at Aberangell upstream eased the amount of traffic over the old bridge. The parapets of the old bridge were rebuilt with the carriageway remaining at 8 feet or 2.4 metres. Unfortunately the Highways Department desecrated the bridge by using sawn pieces of quarry waste. A public outcry did not stop the 'beauty treatment' when cement wash covered the stonework. It is understandable therefore that the bridge is not listed but the place remains beautiful even though the main feature has been ruined.

PONT MINLLYN

Map: Ordnance Survey 1:25,000 Explorer series OL 23 Cadair Idris & Llyn Tegid
Grid reference: SH 859 139

The structure seen today remains impressive as it sits astride the Afon Dyfi at Minllyn close to Dinas Mawddwy. It is under the care of CADW the Welsh Ancient Monuments Society. Fortunately the bridge no longer has traffic passing over it as a modern concrete structure now carries the A470. The bridge was built in 1846 and its original name was Pont Ffinant. The OS map of 1880 shows both names. There was a crossing here in 1678 and in mistake for another bridge close by it was called Pontrusk and was a crossing on the road from Welshpool to Caernarfon.

Although there were other bridges built here a new bridge was constructed in 1635 a new bridge with funds secured by Dr John Davies and what is described in the church records as Pont y Ffynant (note the y in this spelling). The wooden structure was built on three stone pillars. There are a couple of theories why he built this

bridge. One was for the benefit of his parishioners and the other after he had been thrown from his horse whilst fording the river.

In 1813 it was described as an ivy clad bridge of two arches. It had a span of 60 feet or 18.3 metres with a width of 8 feet or 2.4 metres. It was also described as having no parapets. As such it was in a great state of decay. Local pressure enabled some repair work to be undertaken until CADW came to the rescue.

1. Pont Minllyn; 2. Pont Minllyn, looking upstream.

76   *Old Bridges of Snowdonia*

PONT PEN STRYD

Map: Ordnance Survey 1:25,000 Explorer series OL 18 Harlech, Porthmadog & Bala/Y Bala
Grid reference: SH 730 305
Named Pont y Llyn-du on OS maps.

Spanning the Afon Gain this attractive single arch bridge is built with river boulders and looks antiquated. It has been repaired and re-pointed. From the tiny hamlet and chapel at Penystyrd a dead end road is followed for a mile to the bridge. A track close to the road end connects with Gwynfynydd Gold Mine. It has two square flood openings best seen from the downstream side. The width of the road between the 2 feet 6 inches or 76 centimetres high parapets is 10 feet 6 inches or 3.2 metres. This area feels very remote.

1. Pont Pen Stryd looking upstream with flood portals clearly seen;
2. Pont Pen-y-benglog looking downstream;
3. Pont Pen-y-benglog upstream side.

PONT PEN-Y-BENGLOG

Map: Ordnance Survey 1:25,000 Explorer series OL 17 Snowdon/Yr Wyddfa
Grid reference: SH 648 605

The present A5 road bridge close to Idwal Cottage is of 1928 vintage. However, below it and hidden from view from the roadside is a small 18th century single segmental arch bridge built from rubble stone. It can be visited by crossing a stile to the east just below the start of the out-flowing stream. Spanning Afon Ogwen the main bridge seen today is on the site of Telford's bridge built in the 1820's as part of creating the 'turnpike' from London to Holyhead between 1815 and 1830. The Afon Ogwen here is a fine series of waterfalls that crash down into the head of the Nant Ffrancon. Well worth a visit. Care is needed as there is a long drop from the main vantage point. Access is from the west side of the road through a gate.

PONT RHYDLANFAIR

Map: Ordnance Survey 1:25,000 Explorer series OL 18 Harlech, Porthmadog & Bala/Y Bala
Grid reference: SH 827 524

This single arch bridge spans the Afon Conwy before it starts its headlong plunge towards Conwy Falls. Close to the A5 on a minor road the bridge is marked as an antiquity on the OS map. The bridge was built by Robert Griffiths, a local builder, and completed in 1780. It then carried the old road from Ysbyty Ifan to Llanrwst. Two previous attempts to build a bridge here failed. It has a span of 90 feet or 27.4 metres and a width of 15 feet or 4.6 metres. The date of construction is carved in Roman numerals on the upstream 3 feet or 91.5 centimetres high parapet. The coping stones have been 'stapled' together. Although rhyd translates as a ford it is hard to imagine one here in times past.

In 1810 it was described as 'new bridge of one very lofty arch and of a wide span over the Conwy' It is now listed. Unfortunately it has had several repairs quite recently. The wood former for the arch was built in Chester before being transported in sections, much like today, to be erected on site. The haulier was named Thomas Edwards who was better known as Twm o'r Nant.

The two failures were due to natural disasters rather than poor workmanship. Floods were the culprit each time. An 'englyn' was written by John Thomas about Pont Rhydlanfair :

Llun enfys hysbys yw i - llun camog
Llun cwman y milgi;
Llun 'C' uwch cerwyn freci.
Llun cwr lloer yn llyncu'r lli

This translates to:
A bridge in the image of a perfect rainbow, – the image

Of a greyhound bent and hunchbacked;
The image of the letter 'C' above a brewing vat;
The image of a pointed moon swallowing the flow.

An englyn is a traditional Welsh and Cornish short poem. It uses quantitative meters involving counting syllables and rigid patterns of rhyme and half rhyme. each line has a repeating pattern of consonants and accent. Many have been created to celebrate the building of special bridges.

PONT RHYDYDYFRGI

Map: Ordnance Survey 1:25,000 Explorer series OL 18 Harlech, Porthmadog & Bala/Y Bala
Grid reference: SH 847 514

Alternative names for this bridge are Pont Pant Glas and Pont Lima. On the 1:25,000 map it is shown as an antiquity. A plaque with the date of 1862 is placed in the upstream parapet. Usually this dates when a bridge was built, however, it has been said that the bridge was actually built in 1788. So perhaps the date refers to an improvement! It consists of a large single arch over the Afon Conwy with a smaller arch on the true left and is situated in the abutment. A minor road 18 feet wide 5.48 metres wide passes over these ad between parapets 3 feet or 91.5 centimetres high.

1. *Pont Rhydlanfair, downstream side;*
2. *Pont Rhydydyfrgi looking upstream.*

PONT RHYD-Y-GWAIR

Map: Ordnance Survey 1:25,000 Explorer series OL 23 Cadair Idris & Llyn Tegid
Grid reference: SH 798 201

Translates as *hay bridge* whilst 'rhyd' suggests there was a ford here at one time. It spans Afon Celynog on the old route from Brithdir to Llanuwchllyn. It may well have been crossed by Mary Jones when she walked 25 miles from Llanfihangel y Pennant in the Dysynni Valley to Bala in her quest to buy a bible in 1800. She was then only 15 years old. She apparently walked barefoot! It is a single arch rustic looking bridge. The track between the 3 feet 7 inches or 1.09 metres high parapet is only 7 feet 4 inches or 2.24 metres wide. The copings on the parapet are set vertically of random stone.

PONT SARN DDU

Map: Ordnance Survey 1:25,000 Explorer series OL 18 Harlech, Porthmadog & Bala/Y Bala
Grid reference: SH 711 515

Not actually marked on the OS map but the nearby station is called Roman Bridge/Pont Rufenig, but it is old. The station was named thus in the belief it was. Pont Sarn Ddu is not Roman but it is, nevertheless, still very old and is well worth visiting. Spanning the Afon Lledr it is built in the style of a clapper bridge and is a style unique to Dyffryn Lledr. Another is Pont y Pant described later.

The bridge was possibly built without a parapet and the metal one seen today is quite recent having replaced an earlier one. Eight piers with six openings and another four serving as flood portals. At one time the width was 10 feet or 3 metres but is now only 8 feet or 2.4 metres. All in all a remarkable bridge.

1. *Pont Rhyd-y-gwair looking upstream;*
2. *Pont Sarn Ddu.*

PONT SCETHIN

Map: Ordnance Survey 1:25,000 Explorer series OL 18 Harlech, Porthmadog & Bala/Y Bala
Grid reference: SH 634 235

This very remote bridge, at the southern end of the Rhinogydd, spans Afon Ysgethin shortly after it leaves Llyn Bodlyn on its journey to the sea and is some 2½ miles upstream from Pont Fadog. The 8 feet or 2.4 metres rough stone arch over the infant river has parapets of 15 inches or .5 metre. Not only was this a packhorse bridge on the Drovers route to markets in London it was on the old coaching route from Harlech to London via Bont-ddu and Dolgellau. What a dreadful bumpy and scary journey this must have been for the occupants of the carriages never mind the poor horses, especially so when mist obscured the way ahead, when rain teemed down driven by a south westerly gale. The bridge itself is a Scheduled Monument of National importance. Marker stones placed at spaced intervals marked the way over Bwlch y Rhiwgyr.

PONT TAL-Y-BONT

Map: Ordnance Survey 1:25,000 Explorer series OL 18 Harlech, Porthmadog & Bala/Y Bala
Grid reference: SH 687 415

This high single arch bridge spans Afon Cynfal just before its confluence with Afon Dwyryd. Although Afon Cynfal is benign at this point the river has descended tumultuously from the Migneint. It feels somewhat gloomy as the sun rarely reaches into the depths of the wooded gorge. Carrying the A496 fine buttresses support the side walls.

1. Pont Sgethin looking upstream;
2. Pont Tal-y-bont (Cynfal) 2, looking up from downstream;
3. Pont Tal-y-bont (Cynfal) downstream view.

Old Bridges of Snowdonia 83

PONT Y CWRT

Map: Ordnance Survey 1:25,000 Explorer series OL 23 Cadair Idris & Llyn Tegid
Grid reference: SH 675 071

Sometimes referred to as Abergynolwyn bridge which it was known as in the County records of the early 19th century. It is built from stone rubble. The arch is formed from shaped voussoirs rising from slightly outset springers at water level and rises to 7 feet 4 inches or 2.2 metres at its centre. The span is 22 feet or 6.7 metres. There are flush spanderels. The 1 foot 10 inches or .55 metre high parapet sits on top of a string course and the coping is of roughly hewn slate. Interestingly the parapet is constructed from squared rubble in unusually long pieces. The carriageway is 14 feet 6 inches wide or 4.45 metres.

PONT Y GAIN

Map: Ordnance Survey 1:25,000 Explorer series OL 18 Harlech, Porthmadog & Bala/Y Bala
Grid reference: SH 752 328

A single arch bridge that carries the mountain road from Trawsfynydd to Llanuwchllyn spans Afon Gain, a tributary of Afon Mawddach, in a remote area. The bridge is narrow only just allowing cars to cross. During World War II the area was used extensively as an artillery range with much destruction hereabouts. Fortunately the bridge survived with no damage. Unfortunately it was many years after the range closed that the road was re-opened due to the dangers of unexploded shells littering the area. The downstream side of the bridge is a fine picnic site and is also gives the best view of the bridge.

1. *Pont y Cwrt;* 2. *Pont y Foel spanning Afon Foel in Cwm Penmachno;* 3. *Pont y Gain and waterfalls looking upstream.*

PONT Y GARTH

Map: Ordnance Survey 1:25,000 Explorer series OL 23 Cadair Idris & Llyn Tegid
Grid reference: SH 635 070

Spanning Afon Dysynni this is a fine bridge spoilt somewhat by the liberal use of concrete to support the central cutwater. It was built between 1797 and 1798 by David Jones, a stonemason and Richard Roberts, a carpenter for the princely sum of £103! There are two segmented but shallow arches on to a central pier. The parapet is 1 foot 8 inches or .5 metre with horizontal coping stones. At their apex the arches are 9 feet or 2.75 metres above water and each span is 16 feet or 4.9 metres supporting the 15 feet or 4.58 metres carriageway. There is a small refuge in the west parapet.

For those who would rather walk to see this bridge, rather than drive as parking is non-existing a very pleasant one starts at the large lay-by near to Llanllwyda Farm and follows the road below Craig yr Aderyn, *'birds rock'*. Cormorants nest on this cliff due to the fact that the crag was once on the coast. Other birds use this as their nesting ground, Kestrels, Ravens and the rare Chough. The more prominent and lower summit of Craig yr Aderyn has concentric Bronze and Iron-Age fortifications and makes a wonderful viewpoint for the valley and is easily incorporated into the walk if desired.

1. *Pont y Garth, showing the modern downstream rounded cutwater.*

PONT-Y-PAIR

Map: Ordnance Survey 1:25,000 Explorer series OL 17 Snowdon/Yr Wyddfa
Grid reference: SH 791 567

Possibly the most photographed bridge in Snowdonia. A Grade II listed building it spans Afon Llugwy in Betws-y-coed and carries the B5106 to Trefriw. Llugwy is probably and ancient reference to the Celtic God of the sun or light. The view of the cauldron like waterfalls from the bridge is a grand one and often causes traffic congestion with people taking a multitude of pictures. In fact the bridge is literally *the bridge of the cauldron*. There are five segmental arches of differing dimensions. The central arch spans the river. It was partly built by Hywel the *saer maen*, stonemason, who hailed from Bala but he died around 1475 having only completed the downstream side and thus only suitable for packhorses to cross. He made good use of the natural rock shelves for the bridge foundations. The present bridge is probably 17th century but rebuilt in the late 18th or early 19th. In 1797 Sir Richard Colt-Hoare said it was the '

romantic bridge over the River Llugwy' It was described in its present form by Richard Fenton in 1810. The bridge was widened around 1800 making the carriageway 16 feet wide or 5 metres.

Built from stone rubble the length is 148 feet or 45 metres. The voussoirs are roughly dressed and are slightly inset beneath the arch rings formed of narrower stones. The 2 feet 11 inches or 89 centimetres high parapets are also constructed from rubble and are coped with slate slabs.

Betws-y-coed '*Prayer house in the wood*' has been a centre of attraction for centuries. Once a scattered community centred on a packhorse track with tyddyn, '*smallholdings*' scattered around the hillsides. It was said the wood was so dense that a squirrel could travel from Dolgarrog to Dolwyddelan a distance of 14 miles without touching the ground. Much of the forest disappeared to supply wood for smelters furnaces, whilst during the War of the Roses clearings were established for agricultural smallholdings. Potatoes before 1758 were in short supply and had to be brought in but by 1780 there was a surplus and some 13,599 bushels of potatoes were exported from the port of

Conwy. (A bushel is the equivalent in capacity of 8 gallons or 36.4 litres, used for corn, fruit, liquids, etc,).

From 1800 onwards more land was secured from the hillsides during which time Pont-y-pair was improved as traffic had increased. In 1808 the first Irish Mail Coach passed through Betws and in 1815 Waterloo Bridge was built across the Afon Conwy for the London to Holyhead thoroughfare to pass through the village.

As traffic increased more and more people came to marvel at the sights that included Swallow Falls, the various lakes, Fairy Glen and the Miners' Bridge. Scenery around the village is rugged and dramatic adding to its reputation. Hotels sprang up and started taking people on their own excursions including one from the Waterloo taking people on a round trip from Betws-y-coed to Porthmadog, Blaenau Ffestiniog and Dolwyddelan and back to Betws. All this of course using two horse wagons. The advent of both the Conwy Valley Railway line brought many people and as soon as cars were developed even more came to marvel at the scenery. By the turn of the 1800's Betws was assured continuing popularity and has endured even greater popularity since.

1. Pont y Pair upstream view;
2. Pont y Pair, downstream side;
3. Pont y Pandy, Afon Machno looking downstream in flood.

PONT Y PANDY

Map: Ordnance Survey 1:25,000 Explorer series OL 18 Harlech, Porthmadog & Bala/Y Bala
Grid reference: SH 806 529

Marked as a Roman Bridge on the OS map but it definitely isn't. The single arch bridge spans Afon Machno and being somewhat shrouded in greenery it is easy to make the assumption that it has Roman origins, but old it certainly is. The width is a mere 6 feet or 2.4 metres. It has no parapets and is easily seen looking downstream from the more modern road bridge. Pandy waterfalls can be seen a short distance upstream adjacent to the old woollen mill from the upstream side of the road bridge. A fine sight in flood.

PONT Y PANDY

Map: Ordnance Survey 1:25,000 Explorer series OL 254 Lleyn Peninsula East/Pen Llŷn Ardal Ddwyeiniol
Grid reference: SH 549 433

This is a simple bridge spanning the infant Afon Henwy and built in the late 18th or early 19th centuries possibly in connection with Gorseddau slate quarry. Rising starkly and dramatically above the bridge is the Ynysypandy slate mill. A very impressive sight. The single segmental bridge is built from local rubble stone and 7 feet or 2.1 metres above water level. The span is 18 feet or 5.4 metres and supports a 10 feet or 3.1 metres wide carriageway between 1 foot 6 inches or 45 centimetres high parapets.

This mill is of unique design. Normally a mill would be a long single storey building to facilitate easy manoeuvring of heavy slate slabs. Slab here was processed vertically through the mill! No expense was spared in setting up the machine room which ultimately had expensive saws, planers and dressing machinery. It would have seemed sensible for the slate to enter along the upper and middle tramways and

to leave by the lower one but no records appear to be available as to the exact process. Inside the mill is a large gash that accommodated the 26ft or 8 metres overshot waterwheel. The mill specialised in the manufacture of items such as flooring slabs, dairies, troughs and urinals. After the failure of the quarry the mill fell into disuse although some use may have occurred with slate from Prince of Wales quarry in 1875.

Local tradition reports that the mill was used a chapel whilst in 1888 an Eisteddfod was held here. In 1890 the wood floor was lifted and in 1906 the roof and iron framed windows were also taken away. The ruin toady is a Scheduled Ancient Monument.

The first scratchings started in 1807 and offered for sale in 1836. After many owners the lease was bought by a Bavarian mining engineer going by the grand name of Henry Tobias Tschudy von Uster! He maintained his interest here during the lifetime of the quarry although the lease was bought again in 1854 by Robert Gill and John Harris. These two were the prime movers in the development of the quarry. Between 1855 and 1857 £50,000, an inordinate amount of money for the day, was spent on their project.

1. Pont y Pandy, Cwmystradllyn looking up to Ynysypandy slate mill; 2. Pont y Pandy, Cwmystradllyn looking downstream.

PONT-Y-PANT

Map: Ordnance Survey 1:25,000 Explorer series OL 18 Harlech, Porthmadog & Bala/Y Bala
Grid reference: SH 755 538 for the repaired road bridge and SH 745 526 for the footbridge.

The road bridge downstream of the station was at one time the best and oldest example of a lintel or clapper style of bridges in the Lledr valley. This was according to Jervoise when he undertook his survey of UK bridges in the early 1930's. Unfortunately it has undergone modern repair work and now concrete posts and steel girders. However, upstream and just below Dolwyddelan is a fine example of a clapper style bridge.

This too spans Afon Lledr. The wooden section over the river is a recent addition and is used as a path. There is a long line of square flood openings that are at least 125 years old if not older each with a cutwater facing water flowing down. There are no parapets. Eleven of these flood openings are on the true right whilst there are 9 on the true left.

PONT YR AFON GAM

Map: Ordnance Survey 1:25,000 Explorer series OL 18 Harlech, Porthmadog & Bala/Y Bala
Grid reference: SH 746 418

Spanning Afon Gam this single arch bridge is at the road junction of the B4391 and the B4407. The cafe nearby had, at one time, the distinction of being highest petrol station in Wales although no petrol is available today. Downstream of the bridge the Gam flows into Afon Cynfal at the start of that river's 600 feet or 188 metres high plunge in a series of waterfalls known as the Rhaeadr y Cwm. A fine sight. There is a fading inscription on the 2 feet or 61 centimetres high downstream parapet and, as far as I can make out it is D T 1800 F W. The carriageway is 17 feet or 5.18 metres wide. The coping stones are 10 feet 6 inches or 3.2 metres long and over 4 inches or 10 centimetres thick.

1. Pont-y-pant; 2. Pont-y-pant; close up of flood openings construction; 3. Pont yr Afon Gam; 4. Pont Ystumanner spanning the Afon Dysynni near to Abergynolwyn looking upstream.

PONT TWNNEL, BLAENAU FFESTINIOG

Map: Ordnance Survey 1:25,000 Explorer series OL 18 Harlech, Porthmadog & Bala/Y Bala
Grid reference: SH 696 469

'Twnnel Mawr' or the Large Tunnel was built between 1874 and 1879. It is 2¼ miles long and allowed the London and North Western Railway to profit from the transportation of slate. However, it did cause a lot of friction between them and the Ffestiniog Railway. Prior to the official opening three railway workers were killed when pushing their vehicle through the tunnel. A train came from the opposite direction crashing into them. The cost of the tunnel was a staggering amount for those days at £250,000 for the company but the workers paid a much higher price as it is said that at least 12 men died building both the tunnel and the ventilation shafts. Both Oakley and Llechwedd were able to load their slate directly onto the train whilst it was half in and half out of the tunnel. The opening was celebrated by 70 people at the Baltic Hotel at Rhiwbrydir at the northern end of Blaenau Ffestiniog.

The pillars of 'Y Bont Fawr/Y Bont Goch (*'the large or red bridge'*) Viaduct are all that remains of a fine construction. It was built in 1852 to carry waste slate over Afon Barlwyd. There was so much of this waste material that the tip became known as 'Glan y Don'. A mill, ,Pen y Bont', was built on top of the spoil heap. It became known as the *'red bridge'* in a rather macabre way in that the pillars were stained with blood whenever a horse fell over the side!

STEPPING STONES

Map: Ordnance Survey 1:25,000 Explorer series OL 254 Lleyn Peninsula East/Pen Llŷn Ardal Ddwyreiniol
Grid references: SH 531 465 across the Afon Dwyfor in Cwm Pennant and SH 532 421 across Afon Henwy in Cwmystradllyn.

1. Railway tunnel on the Conwy Valley Blaenau Ffestiniog to Llandudno line known as 'Twnnel Fawr'; 2. Stepping Stones across Afon Henwy at the lower end of Cwmystradllyn; 3. Stepping Stones across Afon Dwyfor.

These illustrate examples of early stream crossings. Whilst negotiable in low and normal flow they become dangerous in times of heavy rain when water covers their top surfaces.

VIVIAN QUARRY V2 INCLINE BRIDGE

Map: Ordnance Survey 1:25,000 Explorer series OL 17 Snowdon/Yr Wyddfa
Grid reference: SH 585 605

This bridge is situated beneath the incline and spans the road leading up to the Quarry Hospital. It is dated 1886. Before reaching this another incline bridge spans the road and carries the A1 incline. The V2 incline was completed in 1873 and continued in service until the 1920's. The wagons had a level base and slates were loaded on to one of the wagons. The

loaded wagon travelled down whilst the empty one went up. The incline was restored in 1998. The width of each track is 5'6" or 1.68 metres with both having a gradient of 1:1.3.

WATERLOO BRIDGE

Map: Ordnance Survey 1:25,000 Explorer series OL 17 Snowdon/Yr Wyddfa
Grid reference: SH 798 557

This wonderful bridge is one of Telford's greatest if not the greatest. It spans Afon

1. V2 incline bridge Vivian slate quarry; 2. V2 incline,Vivian slate quarry; 3. Waterloo Bridge looking upstream.

Conwy and carries the A5 into Betws-y-coed. It was also the 7th bridge to be constructed from iron. It was built in 1815 after Napoleon was beaten in Belgium, during the famous 'Battle of Waterloo'. It was known as the Y Hen Haearn, *The Iron Bridge*. It has a span of 108 feet or 33 metres. The pierced spandrels are very ornate being decorated with emblems of Wales, leek; England, rose; Scotland, thistle and Ireland, shamrock. Spanning the whole arch is written ' This arch was constructed in the same year the Battle of Waterloo was fought'. When it was built it

only carried the stagecoaches on the run from London to Holyhead and the Irish mail. With the advent of heavy cars and wagons the bridge was strengthened to support the extra weight.

Waterloo Bridge from the upstream side.

GLOSSARY

ABUTMENT - A solid stone construction that supports the lateral pressure at each end of an arch

ARCH(ES) - The support(s) for the road or track

ARCH RING - A single, or sometimes double, course of stones that form an arch

BALUSTER - Short pillars that support a rail thus forming a balustrade

BRANDER - The foundation for piers.

BUTTRESS - A stone built often tapered block attached to a wall at regularly intervals to strengthen a wall

CLAPPER BRIDGE - A bridge composed of horizontal slabs of stone, often of slate, resting on a rough stone pier. They get their name from the noise they make when the slabs become loose and 'clap' when something passes over them

COPING STONE - Also known as a capstone. Flat stones that cover the tops of parapets providing waterproofing and protection from the weather

CUTWATER - The pointed, or sometimes rounded, face of a bridge pier usually built on the upstream side designed to divide the current of water

ENTABLATURE - A feature supported by columns consisting of an architrave, frieze and cornice

FLOOD OPENINGS OR ARCHES - These were built to relieve pressure on the main arches when the river floods. Often arched they can also have a lintel rather than an arch

FOUNDATIONS - These from the underpinning for abutments and piers. Usually piers were supported by foundations of Branders and Starlings

KEYSTONE - This is the central voussoir of an arch. It is tapered and acts as a lock for the stonework

OGEE or OGEE ARCH - A pointed arch made with an S shaped curve on each side

PARAPET - The protection wall on the bridge helping to stop vehicles and people from falling over

PIER - The load bearing support for the arch

PILASTER - A shallow rectangular column attached to the face of the bridge wall and typically non load bearing

RECESS OR REFUGE - Recesses were built over a cutwater as a safe haven for pedestrians to avoid being knocked over. Usually they are a feature of the 16th century

RUBBLE - Rough hewn stone that was often dressed in the quarry of extraction

SEGMENTED - The arch is the shape of a segment of a circle rather than a full semicircle

SPANDREL - A triangular space usually seen in pairs between the top of an arch and a rectangular frame, between the tops of two adjacent arches or one of the four spaces between a circle within a square. They are frequently filled with decorative features

SPRINGER - The term for the lowest voussoir on each side of an arch. It rests on the pier of the arch, that is, the topmost part of the abutment, from which the arch arises

STARLING - An artificial island underneath a pier and most common in English bridges

STRING COURSE - Otherwise known as Belt course or Band Course. It is the horizontal row of masonry, narrower than the other courses that extend across the length of the bridge below the parapet

VOUSSOIR(S) - Wedge shaped stones that make up the arch ring. Two are of greater importance than the others, the keystone and springer

1. *Barmouth Bridge looking towards Cadair Idris;* 2. *Pont Llanelltyd looking upstream;* 3. *Pont Pen Stryd, looking downstream;* 4. *Bont Newydd, Abergwyngregyn looking downstream.*

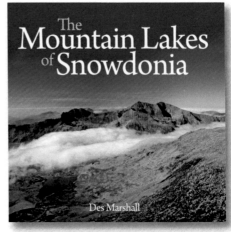

The Mountain Lakes of Snowdonia

Des Marshall

Snowdonia's Waterfalls
Des Marshall

Snowdonia Slate
The story with photographs
Des Marshall

Day Walks FROM THE Slate Trail of Snowdonia
Des Marshall

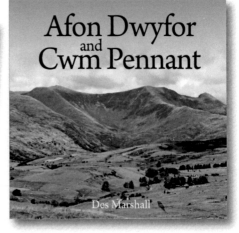

Afon Dwyfor and Cwm Pennant

Des Marshall